The BOOK of REVELATION TODAY

The BOOK of REVELATION TODAY

New Insights for Last Days Survival

Farley Anderson

COPYRIGHT © 1994 BY
HORIZON PUBLISHERS & DISTRIBUTORS, INC.

All rights reserved. Reproduction in whole or any parts thereof in any form or by any media without written permission is prohibited.

First Printing, November 1994

International Standard Book Number
0-88290-505-8

Horizon Publishers' Catalog and Order Number
1044

Printed and distributed
in the United States of America by

Horizon Publishers
& Distributors, Incorporated
P.O. Box 490 Bountiful, Utah 84011-0490

Acknowledgments

This book is dedicated with love and gratitude to John the Beloved, who yet walks among us. Thank you, John, for a love so pure that you have chosen to be with the people to the end (D & C 7).

Special thanks are expressed to Helen, my wife, whose love and support are unending, who always believed I could do it, and who has carried a double load of family responsibilities when the pen, research, or even a mighty wrestle with an idea, would call, often at the most unusual hours. Others, without whom this book could not have been written, are:

Joe Sampson, who came into my life and has acted as a mentor during the process of writing this book. Joe's gospel background, knowledge of Hebrew and ancient languages and cultures, friendship, and most of all his ear, have all been greatly appreciated;

Larry, who encouraged me to put my thoughts into book form and also gave feedback and ideas;

Kit Kartchner, for special help with the research and editing of the book;

Valerie Stewart, for typing, and also contributing during that process;

And lastly, my parents, who taught me never to be afraid to think a new thought, to march to the beat of a different drummer, to do the right thing regardless, and who have always been there with love and support.

Special thanks to Duane Crowther, Lorin May, and the staff at Horizon Publishers for direction and technical help, and for rapidly putting the book into production.

Introduction

Many people view the events prophesied to take place in the last days from a position of fear and nebulous understanding that borders on panic. To these, the message of this book is "Repent." The Lord has great need of men and women of courage, understanding, and faith as we enter the most exciting, interesting, and climactic period of the earth's history.

The scriptural analogy given to describe our present time is the likeness of a woman taken in travail (John 16:21). This type is very fitting, for each individual's experience is universal, yet unique. To the unprepared, unwed mother, who has spent nine months in denial, guilt, and riotous living, the experience of delivery is dreaded and even dangerous (1 Thessalonians 5:2-3). Panic often accompanies her fear of the unknown and makes labor and delivery even worse. She may even consider terminating life—the new life within her, or even her own. On the other hand, to the prepared woman clothed in virtue, full of faith, surrounded by the love and support of family, friends, and seraphic hosts of the eternal worlds, who knows herself and has studied the combined wisdom of the ages in relationship to her delivery, the price is small, the bitter pill short-lived, the glory eternal, and the moment of delivery most spectacular.

The great and dreadful day of the Lord will be great to some and dreadful to others. Our individual experience will be determined by where we stand in relation to him whose coming we await. The perspective from the mountain top is vastly different from that of the ditch. Let us rise up without fear and prepare to meet the Lord!

In former dispensations, the prophets have rejoiced when they were shown our day in vision. They have called this time period before the Savior comes again a great and dreadful day (Malachi 4:5). The last days have been compared by the Savior to the time of Noah (Matthew 24:37), contrasted by the designated time of the Marvelous Work and a Wonder (Isaiah 29:14). It is a time not only of fullness, but also a day when even the elect, if it were possible, are deceived and Satan rules over his own (Matthew 24:24). It is in our day that we can live out the Chinese curse and blessing, "May you live in interesting times."

We who live in this time have been given the opportunity, blessing, and calling to be the Lord's people and to bring forth Zion, that city set upon a hill. The words of John reach across the centuries to Saints in modern days, and urge us to forsake Babylon and to prepare to meet our Savior. With the help of the scriptures and the teachings of the prophets, we will not be found walking in darkness at noonday. The Book of Mormon and Doctrine and Covenants give great insight into the Book of Revelation; indeed, the Book of Revelation reads like a condensation of these books. Isaiah, Daniel, Ezekiel, Jeremiah, Matthew, and other biblical writers also address last-day subjects, but nowhere is so much last-day prophecy gathered in one place.

This book is based on the premise that the Revelation of John provides an actual symbolic model of the real world in which we live today. The approach of the author is as follows:

- We live in the last days, and since much of the book describes this time period, we are not only justified in likening the scriptures to us, but commanded to. This day and this scripture are meant for each other. Joseph Smith said: "The things which John saw had no allusion to the days of Adam, Enoch, Abraham, or Jesus, only so far as is plainly represented by John . . . John saw only that which was lying in futurity and which was shortly to come to pass (*Teachings of the Prophet Joseph Smith*, p. 289).
- John, after seeing our day, wrote what was most valuable to enable us to recognize and separate ourselves from Satan. The Book of Revelation contains major keys to recognize Satan, his works, and his earthly kingdom in these last days; understanding these keys will enable us to avoid being deceived.
- By tying the words of John to the other scriptures and to the words of our modern prophets, we will obtain a clear picture of current affairs and the world around us.
- The foundation for what is going to happen in the near future has already been laid. The tree has been planted and is growing, though it may not bear its fruit for yet a little season. Once we understand the prophecies, we will more easily recognize the means that will bring them about.

What is the Book of Revelation, and why is it important that we study and understand it? John saw our day in vision, and then he carefully wrote his vision in such a way that the Saints who would live in this day could discover truths necessary to overcome the trials and plagues that would come, and then rise triumphantly to meet the Savior. Much of John's mission, to gather and separate the righteous of the twelve tribes of Israel from the "Babylonian" world in the last days, depends on our understanding what he has written for us; those who study and understand his words will joyfully and easily gather and separate themselves from the world.

Indeed, perhaps the time of the Second Coming hinges on the righteous earnestly seeking to understand John's prophecy and revelation of the events that will usher it in. The Brother of Jared also saw what John saw in vision. Moroni, who read the account of this magnificent vision, tells us that "there never were greater things made manifest than those which were made manifest unto the brother of Jared" (Ether 4:4). He was commanded by the Lord to write this awe-inspiring vision, and he did so, but was restrained from giving it to us. Moroni promises latter-day readers that it will be made available to us, but only on certain conditions:

> Behold, when ye shall rend that veil of unbelief which doth cause you to remain in your awful state of wickedness, and hardness of heart, and blindness of mind, then shall the great and marvelous things which have been hid up from the foundation of the world from you—yea, when ye shall call upon the Father in my name, with a broken heart and a contrite spirit, then shall ye know that the Father hath remembered the covenant which he made unto your fathers, O house of Israel.
>
> And then shall my revelations which I have caused to be written by my servant John be unfolded in the eyes of all the people. *Remember, when ye see these things, ye shall know that the time is at hand that they shall be made manifest in very deed.*
>
> (Ether 4:15-16)

Moroni was not allowed to unfold to the eyes of all the people what John had written. Perhaps more chapters in the Book of Revelation will yet be given to us; or perhaps the understanding of what John wrote is given to one at a time, when we as individuals are ready to receive it, and understanding is confirmed by the testimony of the Spirit. We must each offer to Christ in sacrifice our own heart, broken by the recognition of our sins and the price he paid to redeem us from them; our spirit, contritely willing to relinquish our selfish pride to his will for our lives. We must freely give up our favorite temptations and wickedness in order to live as he has asked us to live. We must let go of pre-conceived notions, long-held traditions and beliefs that have kept us hard-hearted and blinded to truth, and be willing to cast off our unbelief. We must "rend that veil of unbelief" and believe things that may be hard to believe. Our hunger to know must impel us to our knees, where we call upon the Father in earnest prayer for this knowledge to be unfolded to our hearts. Only then will the truth of John's vision be "unfolded" to our eyes.

It may be useful for the reader to understand the process the author used in seeking to understand John's writing. The study of the Book of Revelation began in earnest a few years back, prompted by the realization that understanding it was a requisite to understanding the last days. A major key to unlocking this work is knowing that the English word *revelation* is translated from the Greek word *apocalypse*, which means to make known or to uncover. When John's writings are read with this in mind, the images seem to jump out of the pages and hold us spellbound. The book was prayerfully studied from this perspective, often remembering that John wanted to make these things known to us. In immersed study, the text, the setting, the types, and the personalities were absorbed. It was felt that if we could just get a clear picture of who was doing what, then the story line would be easier to follow. On paper, the characters were mapped out and their attributes listed. In pondering these images, and by approaching the scriptures from the perspective that John was trying to teach us, and not confuse us, in amazement came the recognition of the characters John was describing. The first character to unveil his identity, through a careful study of his revealed attributes, was the "Scarlet Beast." By putting a few more of the pieces of the puzzle where it was felt they ought to fit, testing was begun to see if understanding was achieved from this model, and if the other pieces described by John would fit in place next to them. This study proved enlightening. The results were shared with others, and the value of a work such as this became apparent. At the prodding of a friend in the publishing business, the author began this book.

Much additional light has come to the author since that initial study period. There have been times when the information seemed to flow and almost write itself. At other times, great effort and thorough research had to be used to interpret and confirm the images John gives us. This book was created from the knowledge that the purpose of John's revelation is not to hide or keep knowledge hidden, but to make things known, and to help us see the world in which we now live from the heavenly vantage point. The author believes that the Book of Revelation is much simpler than it is usually made out to be; it is complex only if we try to make it into something that it is not.

If what is written causes people to study, to think and ponder, to pray, and to form opinions, then this book has certainly fulfilled its purpose. With no apologies, this book will attempt to communicate the reality of our world as described by John. The opinions are those of the author; full responsibility is taken for them. The hope is that what is written may be of value in your search for truth, but it is also recognized that salvation is an individual matter. A prayer is offered that what is written will first and foremost be acceptable and in accordance with the will of him of whose coming we seek. May all of us rise to the wonderful challenge and adventure that await us.

Contents

Acknowledgments **7**
Introduction **8**
Suggestions for Reading this Book **18**

1 Promises, Blessing, and Testimony of Christ **19**
   The Character of John the Revelator 19
   The Importance of the Book of Revelation 21

2 The Church Faces Judgment **24**
   Ephesus 24
   Smyrna 24
   Pergamos 24
   Thyatira 25

3 The Judgment Continues **26**
   Sardis 26
   Philadelphia 26
   Laodiceans 26
   Christian or Pro-Christ Attributes
      in the Early Church 27
   Anti-Christ Attributes in the Early Church 27
   Promises unto the Repentant and Righteous 28

4 The Celestial World Described **30**
   Latter-day Revelation on John's Prophecies 30

5 Salvation of Man and Beast **32**
   Animals to Partake of Salvation 32
   The Salvation of Men 33

6 The Earth's First 6,000 Years **35**
   Seal Number 1 35
   Verse 2 35
   Seal Number 2 35
   Verse 4 35

	Seal Number 3	36
	Verses 5-7	36
	Seal Number 4	36
	Verse 8	36
	Seal Number 5	37
	Verses 9-11	37
	Understanding the Atonement	37
	Conditions for Blessings of the Atonement	37
	Sacrifice Required of the Lord	40
	Seal Number 6	40
	Verses 12-17	40
7	**Tribulation and the Sixth Seal**	**42**
	The Holding of Four Winds	42
	The Sealing of 144,000	43
	The Blessings of Great Tribulation	45
	Likening Enoch to the Last Days	45
	Lessons from Enoch's Teaching	47
	The Lord Protects His People	48
8	**The Seven Latter-day Plagues**	**51**
	The Opening of the Seventh Seal	51
	One Theory About Heaven's Silence	52
	Prophecy of Seven Great Plagues	53
	Woes of the Seventh Seal	54
	The Destructions in Modern-day Terms	55
	Wormwood—a Modern Parallel	56
	Other Precautions Against the Plague	58
	Protections Against Nuclear Contamination	59
9	**Two Great World Conflicts**	**61**
	Environmentalism Used for Evil Purposes	61
	Army of 200 Million Assembled	62
10	**John's Mission to Heirs of Salvation**	**64**
	The Angel Who Ends Telestial Time	64
	The Time of the Second Coming	66

11 Jerusalem's Prophets, Destruction and Deliverance ... 70
  Two Prophets with Great Power ... 70
  Four Woes May Bypass Jerusalem ... 71
  A Temple in Jerusalem ... 72
  Two Cities Caught Up to Heaven ... 73
  Melchizedek as a Type of the Second Coming ... 74

12 Satan's Earthly Kingdoms ... 76
  The Personality of Satan ... 77
  The Church Flees to the Wilderness ... 78
  A Lesson from the Colonization of America ... 78
  Only the Righteous Should Govern ... 79
  Look to a System's Fruits ... 80

13 The Image and Mark of the Beast ... 84
  Understanding Symbols of the Beast ... 84
  The Earthly Identity of the Beast ... 85
  Wounding and Healing of the Beast ... 86
  A Second Beast Speaks to the World ... 87
  The Beasts Flourish Today ... 90
  Joseph Smith ... 91
  Brigham Young ... 91
  John Taylor ... 91
  Wilford Woodruff ... 92
  Lorenzo Snow ... 92
  Joseph F. Smith ... 93
  Heber J. Grant ... 93
  George Albert Smith ... 93
  David O. McKay ... 94
  Joseph Fielding Smith ... 94
  Harold B. Lee ... 95
  Spencer W. Kimball ... 95
  Ezra Taft Benson ... 96
  The Image, Mark, and Number of the Beast ... 97
  A Possible Fulfillment of the Mark ... 102
  Understanding the Number of the Beast ... 105
  America Has Strayed From the Constitution ... 107

14	The Harvesting of the Earth	109
15	Victory Over Plagues for the Righteous	113
	The Coming of Two Cities from Heaven	113
	Jacob and the City of Salem	114
16	Destruction and Plagues for the Wicked	117
	Possible Identity of the False Prophet	118
	The Works of Unclean Spirits	119
17	Satan's Power Broker Exposed	122
	The Great Whore	122
	The Fruits of the Federal Reserve	123
	Today's Wine of Fornication	125
	The Woman's Thirst for Blood	127
	The Unpopular Conspiracy Theories	129
	The Whore and Beast Grow in Power	132
18	Babylon is Destroyed	134
	The Destruction of Ancient Babylon	134
	The Destruction of Present Babylon	135
19	Preparation for the Marriage Supper	137
20	Satan Banished as the Millennium Begins	139
21	The Righteous Enter Christ's Presence	141
22	The Holy City	144
	Conclusion	146
	Appendix A	151
	Author's Condensed Interpretive Historical Perspective of the World from the Time of Christ	151
	Christ's Work and Glory	151
	Satan's Dominion	151
	The Rise to Power of the Whore Babylon	151
	Satan's Influence Increases under Communism and Socialism Communism	153
	Socialism	153

CONTENTS

Appendix B **154**
    Author's Interpretive Chronology of Some Signs and
        Events Prophesied from the Revelation of St. John 154

Appendix C **158**
    Satan's Control vs. God's Agency and Protection 158
    Lucifer's "Ifs" to Gain Control 158
    Christ's "Truth" to Make Us Free 158

Appendix D **162**
    An Enemy Hath Done This: The Threat to Our Freedom ... 162

Bibliography **166**
    Selected Additional Recommended Reading 169
    Political Commentary for Today 169
    Special Helps for Predaredness 170

Index **172**

NOTE—Since the chapters of this book correspond to the chapters in the Book of Revelation, the Bible, its indexes, concordances, dictionaries, and lexicons can also be useful to locate treatments of specific topics by chapter.

Suggestions for Reading this Book

A. The Book of Revelation was given to us by God, through John. It will be understood only if we receive that same spirit by which it was given. Moroni gives us the formula for understanding truth through the Holy Ghost, who will teach us the truth of "all things" (Moroni 10:3-5). He exhorts us first to remember how merciful the Lord has been in the past. In this spirit of remembrance, we should always be filled with thankfulness and gratitude. Thanks should be given to God for sending his Son, about whose testimony the Book of Revelation was written; for the gift of the scriptures he has given to teach us; for John and the other prophets whose charity and service have been in our behalf. We appreciate the promise that even in adversity, if we will search diligently, pray always, walk uprightly and be believing, all things will work together for our good (D & C 90:24). We know of his love, grace, blessings, and salvation; and the knowledge that even the hard and difficult days ahead can work for our good.

B. In meditation and gratitude, we are to ask with a sincere heart through earnest prayer, "in the name of Christ, if these things are not true . . . . And by the power of the Holy Ghost ye may know the truth of all things" (Moroni 10:3-5).

C. Each chapter of the text corresponds with the same numbered chapter in Revelation. This book is written in the form of a companion study guide to the Book of Revelation. The study of this text will prove far more profitable if the text of this book and the text of Revelation are read, studied, pondered, and compared side by side. Read from the inspired scripture. Make mental notes, ponder, and invite the Spirit to open the eyes of your understanding. Be particularly open to how the Book of Revelation applies to you and your life. The Spirit will bring to light gems of truth especially for you.

D. Return to the scriptures. Use the Spirit to confirm or deny your understanding.

1
Promises, Blessings, and Testimony of Christ

The prophet Joseph Smith said, "The book [Revelation] is one of the plainest books God ever caused to be written" (*Teachings of the Prophet Joseph Smith,* p. 290). Of course, John knew that he had to write in such a way that when his writing passed "through the hands of the great and abominable church" (1 Nephi 13:28-29), that church would leave most of his book intact so that the righteous could recognize and use his divine foresight. His job was made somewhat easier because the wicked, in their pride, seldom recognize their own wickedness. When the prophet Nathan testified of King David's great sin, it was not until Nathan told David, "Thou art the man" (2 Samuel 12:7), that he recognized fully what he had done and repentance could begin. The Book of Revelation does not couch its call to repentance in gentle or tactful terms. Like David, we also may need to cry some bitter tears. The book testifies that Christ will come to a people who are prepared to meet him. The trials described are those necessary to bring about that preparation.

The Character of John the Revelator

In looking over the words of John, one can begin to see what kind of person he is. It has often been said that the words of John are the words of love. Charity, defined in the Book of Mormon as the pure love of Christ, is probably the one attribute which best describes John. John is so filled with charity that he is referred to as the disciple that Jesus loved (John 13:23; 19:26; 20:2; 21:20-24). Can you imagine the love that motivated him to request around a 2000-year extension of his difficult mission, especially when he knew firsthand the blessings awaiting him in the mansions prepared by his close personal friend, our Savior?

John received the name "Boanerges" from the Lord, which means Son of Thunder. This is a fitting name for the zealous disciple who was the only one to stay by the Savior's side in one of his darkest earthly hours as he entered the illegal court of the Sanhedrin. Thunder is also a fitting description for the power of John's words. It appears from the record that John had the clearest vision of who the Savior is. It is interesting that he alone begins his gospel with a description of Christ's premortal state, describing him as God, and in the beginning with God, and the creator of all things (John 1:1 and D & C 93).

John also appears to have the clearest vision to recognize the work of the enemy on the earth, both in his day and ours. John was the only one of the original twelve apostles who was privileged to be given a divinely guided tour of the history of this earth and the people on it. He was allowed to ask his heavenly guide questions and to extend teaching in some areas. There is record of only a few other prophets having similar experiences, including Moses, Daniel, the Brother of Jared, Abraham, Lehi, and Nephi. Nephi desired to leave a record of his experience, but the Lord forbade him to write any more, telling him that a later prophet, named John, had been given the mission to leave this testimony:

> And it came to pass that the angel spake unto to me, saying: Look!
>
> And I looked and beheld a man, and he was dressed in a white robe.
>
> And the angel said unto me: Behold one of the twelve apostles of the Lamb.
>
> Behold, he shall see and write the remainder of these things; yea, and also many things which have been.
>
> And he shall also write concerning the end of the world.
>
> Wherefore, the things which he shall write are just and true; and behold they are written in the book which thou beheld proceeding out of the mouth of the Jew; and at the time they proceeded out of the mouth of the Jew, or, at the time the book proceeded out of the mouth of the Jew, *the things which were written were plain and pure, and most precious and easy to the understanding of all men.*
>
> And behold, the things which this apostle of the Lamb shall write are many things which thou hast seen; and behold, the remainder shalt thou see.
>
> But the things which thou shalt see hereafter thou shalt not write; for the Lord God hath ordained the apostle of the Lamb of God that he should write them.
>
> And also others who have been, to them hath he shown all things, and they have written them; and they are sealed up to come forth in

their purity, according to the truth which is in the Lamb, in the own due time of the Lord, unto the house of Israel.

And I, Nephi, heard and bear record, that the name of the apostle of the Lamb was John, according to the word of the angel.

And behold, I, Nephi, am forbidden that I should write the remainder of the things which I saw and heard; wherefore the things which I have written sufficeth me; and I have written but a small part of the things which I saw.

(1 Nephi 14:18-28)

The Importance of the Book of Revelation

President Ezra Taft Benson was beloved for calling the Church to repentance for having too lightly esteemed the precious record left in the Book of Mormon. He urged all members of the Church to spend time daily studying in this great book. Since Nephi directs the reader to the Bible to read the remainder of his vision in John's writings, one must mentally insert John's book into the middle of First Nephi in order to have the whole story. One must study the Book of Revelation as an integral part of the Book of Mormon. Might the saints not be under the same condemnation for ignoring John's written vision as for taking the Book of Mormon too lightly?

John begins his account in the first verse of chapter 1 by testifying to the importance of studying his revelation. He bears witness that:

1. It is the revelation of Jesus Christ. Its purpose is to enable people to know the Savior better. This should be the main reason for studying the Revelation of John.
2. It is given for his servants. In other words, it is a tool chest of knowledge and wisdom to help accomplish this last days-mission.
3. It will teach things that must "shortly come to pass."

John pronounces a blessing in verse 3 on those who will take the time to read and understand the words of his prophecy and keep in their hearts and lives the lessons learned, for the Savior is coming quickly. Whenever a scriptural blessing is pronounced, one should always search for the requirements necessary to claim that blessing (D & C 130:20-21). In this verse, the blessings are not specified, though the method of claiming them is very clear.

One must read, hear, understand (Joseph Smith Translation, Revelation 1:3), and keep the things written therein. Why? Because the time is at hand. He alludes to the blessings as he bears solemn testimony of the reality of the atonement (verse 5), the reward of being made kings and priests (verse 6), and of the promised coming of the Lord Jesus Christ in glory and in the clouds of heaven (verse 7). At this moment, every eye shall see him, but the glory of this coming to all is overshadowed by the joy of the promised experience of the Lord coming to each person individually. The full nature of these marvelous promises will be unfolded in a journey through the exciting pages of The Book of Revelation.

Moses gives insight into the tremendous knowledge John must have received with this vision. When he explained the nature of his revelatory experience, Moses detailed the discerning power attendant to such a manifestation:

> And it came to pass, as the voice was still speaking, Moses cast his eyes and beheld the earth, yea, even all of it; and there was not a particle of it which he did not behold, discerning it by the spirit of God.
> (Moses 1:27)

Imagine seeing the earth with such visionary power as to behold and comprehend every particle of the earth and every soul upon it. Moses 1:35 goes on to reveal that Moses' account included the earth and all its inhabitants. The Lord promises that to those who are faithful, the Spirit will eventually teach all things. The truth that will eventually set a person free includes knowledge of things as they are, and as they were, and as they shall be (D & C 93:24). As one proves faithful in a few things with which the Lord has blessed him, he proves that he can be faithful with the many things with which the Lord wishes to bless him. Revelation 1:6 states that the faithful will be made "both kings and priests unto God." In the eternal realm, political power and spiritual glory and dominion are combined. This condition is the fullness of God's kingdom on earth as it is in heaven—when righteousness prevails in both arenas. Because Satan is opposed to every part of Christ's work, look for his hand to be manifest in both spiritual and political arenas.

In verse 9, John addresses the reader as his brother, and acknowledges that of necessity, this life includes both tribulation and patience.

Verse 10 is the beginning of the actual revelation. John says that the vision came to him as he was in the spirit. In other words, John was prepared to receive. The same spirit is necessary to anyone who wishes to understand John's writing. The vision occurred on the Lord's day. The term *Lord's day* appears only twice in scripture. The first is here in Revelation 1:10, the second is D & C 59:12. Scholars have noted that early Christian writers make no reference to the sabbath or Sunday as the Lord's day. Instead, the term is reserved for the day of the Lord's resurrection (occurring on a Sunday), but mostly, the looked-for day of his second coming. Christ taught that he is the Lord of the Sabbath (Mark 3:2, Luke 6:7). In latter-day revelation the Lord declared that Sunday is the Lord's day (D & C 59:21). The seven-day week ending with a sabbath is a type of the earth's six one-thousand year periods, followed by a one-thousand year millennium reigned over by Christ. It is not known if this scripture reference in Revelation is to John's spiritual experience of the day of the Lord's coming, or if the vision simply occurred on the new sabbath, or both. John was commanded (verse 11) to write and to distribute this work by the voice of the Lord.

John first beholds what looks like seven golden candlesticks. Upon closer examination, he sees that they are personages clothed in glory; they are seven great light givers. In the midst of the seven is one like unto the Son of Man. There are seven dispensations of time, and each is presided over by a presiding prophet, who holds the keys of that dispensation, so a logical assumption is that John is beholding those prophets with Christ in their midst (Revelation 1:13-20). Note that the Joseph Smith Translation clarifies in verse 20 that the seven golden candlesticks are the *servants of the seven churches* and not the churches themselves. In John's day a likeness to this eternal reality is seen with the naming of the seven churches in Asia. Christ testifies of his power over mankind's two greatest enemies, death and hell.

2
The Church Faces Judgment

Chapter 2 begins with the judgments of Christ bearing witness to the spiritual condition of the churches existing in John's day. Church members today should take heed from these examples and admonitions, for the various ways of being overcome by Satan are clearly illustrated, and the same challenges and standards apply. The Lord's promises for those who endure and overcome faithfully are described in this chapter, and are held out to all Latter-day Saints:

Ephesus

This is a church where labor and patience have been borne for Jesus's name. They have been plagued with internal apostasy, led by evil false apostles. Their works have testified against them, and much damage has been done. Although this church has not partaken of the dynamic apostasy and sexual sin associated with the Nicolaitans, if they do not return to their former works they will not have an eternal place with Christ.

Smyrna

Christ begins by testifying that he has overcome death. Though the people suffer tribulation and poverty, they are blessed with the riches of eternity. The fallen state of the Jews is highlighted by the title "synagogue of Satan." The persecution of the saints by the false religion of the day is compounded by the forceful arm of government. The Lord emphasizes that he expects his own to be faithful even unto death. He promises power to those so faithful, and that they will not be overcome by the second death.

Pergamos

Here Zion and the world cannot co-exist. John refers to the place as "Satan's seat." Sexual sin and idolatry are practiced even among church members. Those who overcome, like Antipas, who is commended as a faithful martyr, will eat of the hidden manna or the Bread of Life, which is a symbol of partaking of Christ's power and glory, and will eventually receive their own Urim and Thummim:

> Then the white stone mentioned in Revelation 2:17, will become a Urim and Thummim to each individual who receives one, whereby things pertaining to a higher order of kingdoms will be made known;
>
> And a white stone is given to each of those who come into the celestial kingdom, whereon is a new name written, which no man knoweth save he that receiveth it. The new name is the key word.
>
> (D & C 130:10-11; see also D & C 93)

Thyatira

Christ acknowledges that slowly the conversion has taken place; and now works, charity, service, faith and patience have been manifest. Their problem has been the acceptance of a false prophetess. The foundation of the church has not been doctrinally or spiritually sound, and the members' seduction by false doctrine has been followed by actual physical seduction of priesthood leaders. Many were unaware of the depths of this deception, and Christ tells them to hold fast to the basic doctrines of the church. Those who overcome the onslaught of false doctrine are promised that they will be able to use the rod of iron to be rulers over nations. In the Book of Mormon, Nephi's vision teaches us that the rod of iron is a symbol for the Word of God (see also Joseph Smith Translation, Revelation 2:27). A foundation in Christ's word, sufficient to overcome false doctrine, appears to be a requisite to being a ruler in the hereafter. John is the disciple who used The Word of God as another name for Christ (John 1:1). Those who take Christ's name upon themselves must receive the ordinances and principles of the gospel and strive to become like him, to attain exaltation and be rulers, kings and priests to the most High God.

3
The Judgment Continues

In this chapter, John continues describing the judgements upon the early churches, then lists many promises unto the righteous who endure:

Sardis

The spirit here is already dead; only the form remains. The saints are commanded to be watchful over and strengthen what is left, for their works are not perfect before God. Note that even here, in the weakest of the seven churches, the members are not told to tear down or destroy what remains of the church, or start a new church. Rather, they are commanded to hold fast to the truth and repent. If they are not watchful, they will not be ready to receive Christ. Even here among the weakest of the seven churches, a few remain worthy and not defiled to walk with Christ.

Philadelphia

Christ has opened the door that is beyond the power of man to shut. The saints have used their little strength to valiantly bear witness, and have not denied the name of Christ. Because of this faithfulness, Christ promises that he will keep them from the power of temptation. The covenant illustrated here is that to those who will not be ashamed to take upon them and keep the name of Christ, his name will remain upon them. When his city, the city of God, or New Jerusalem, comes down out of heaven, the door will open to that city.

Laodiceans

The apostasy here is a result of mediocrity. While other churches have faced internal and external persecutions, the people here have been tried, as many saints of the last days are now being tried, with ease and wealth. This physical condition has caused spiritual blindness (Revelation 3:17). The remedy prescribed is to trade what one has for what Christ has, or buy of him the riches of eternity, thereby regaining eternal perspective.

The words of Christ to the Church in ancient times tell what traps to avoid in modern days. One learns what pleases Christ and receives a list of his covenants to the Church, and not the world generally.

As a summary, the author will restate the attributes found among the Church as given in chapters 2 and 3. By grouping the attributes into the following three areas, one can more clearly see the strengths, weaknesses, and promised blessings of the early Christian Church:

Christian or Pro-Christ Attributes in the Early Church

- Works, labor, patience in adversity, not fainting
- works, bearing tribulation in poverty, being faithful unto death
- being a faithful martyr
- holding fast to the name of Christ
- repentance, works, charity, service, faith, patience, not knowing the depths of Satan or accepting his speech, being watchful and strengthening the things of Christ that remain
- remembering the words of Christ already received
- holding fast, repenting, not defiling garments (temple covenants)
- using what little strength one has to hold Christ's word and not deny Christ's name
- keeping the word with patience
- opening the door so that Christ can come into one's life to sup with him

Anti-Christ Attributes in the Early Church

- False apostles who are liars
- a place where false religion (synagogue of Satan) is combined with the force of government (the devil will cast you into prison)
- partaking of the false religion of the day (eating things sacrificed to idols)
- committing fornication
- accepting seductive practices that lead to fornication (the doctrine of the Nicolaitans), which thing Christ hates
- being open to false prophets with seductive practices (the prophetess Jezebel)

- fornication, having the name of Christ, but being dead spiritually
- imperfect works before God
- not watching to know what hour Christ will come
- being lukewarm in the gospel, substituting material wealth and ease for spiritual wealth and Christ's blessings
- being spiritually wretched, miserable, poor, blind, and naked

Promises unto the Repentant and Righteous

- Eating of the tree of life in the midst of the paradise of God
- a crown of Life
- not being hurt by the second death
- eating of the hidden manna
- a personal Urim and Thummim
- a new name
- power over nations
- being a ruler with the rod of iron (the Word of God)
- the morning star
- clothed in a white raiment
- named in the Book of Life
- Christ to personally confess the names of the righteous before the Father and angels
- being kept from the hour of temptation
- Christ coming quickly
- no man to close the door Christ has opened
- no man to take away the crown of the righteous
- being constantly within the temple of God
- being given the name of God
- living in the city of God, the New Jerusalem, which cometh down out of heaven
- Christ to personally come in and sup with him, and he with Christ (Second Comforter!)
- sitting with Christ upon his throne with the Father

One who knows he is loved by Christ can expect his corrective rebuke and chastening and call to repentance. Whomever heeds the Master's call can claim the blessing by covenant of an actual personal relationship with Christ, or a sure calling and election. Following Christ means that one must overcome, even as he overcame, to sit with Christ where he is seated. It is up to every soul to hear the words and feel the spirit of this message given so long ago, as if they were given today (Revelation 3:19-22).

4
The Celestial World Described

It must have been heartbreaking for John to witness Christ's description of the state of apostasy of the church on earth. Father Lehi teaches Jacob in 2 Nephi 2 the importance of opposition, of knowing the bitter to experience the sweet. One can only imagine how sweet it was as John then beheld the Celestial World and the throne of God. Chapter 4 contrasts the earthly church and heavenly fruits of the eternal gospel. Verse 4 of the King James version says that four and twenty elders are sitting around the throne of God; the Joseph Smith Translation clarifies that they are in the midst of the throne. This is in keeping with the promise in Revelation 3:21, where the righteous who overcome the world are promised to be able to sit on the throne with Christ.

Latter-day Revelation on John's Prophecies

In D & C 77, Joseph Smith is given the opportunity to ask questions of an angelic being (perhaps even John himself) about the Revelation of John. Verse 5 shows who these elders are:

> Q. What are we to understand by the four and twenty elders, spoken of by John?
> A. We are to understand that these elders whom John saw, were elders who had been faithful in the work of the ministry and were dead; who belonged to the seven churches, and were then in the paradise of God.
> (D & C 77:5)

Without the revelation given in D & C 77, understanding of this section would be incomplete. The throne of God appears to be a busy and interesting place. Before the throne is a sea of glass, which D & C 77:1 clarifies is the earth in its sanctified, immortal and eternal state. Around the throne are four beasts. D & C 77:2 clarifies that these are actual beasts, symbolically represent ing the eternal salvation and happiness of all of God's creatures. The eyes mentioned in verse 8 represent the light and knowledge; the wings, the power to move and act. The whole tone of this chapter is worshipful, reverent, and awe-inspiring. John tries to give a taste of the glories of eternities that await those who faithfully endure and overcome the trials he introduces in the following chapters of his revelation.

5
Salvation of Man and Beast

Animals to Partake of Salvation

Further knowledge of the salvation of God's creatures is given in Revelation 5, probably the most clear scriptural reference on the subject. Here John sees not only many angels around the throne, but numberless beasts in their resurrected, glorified, and perfected state. Every creature is given the gift of language to worship Christ and say, "Blessings, honour, and glory, and power to him that sitteth upon the throne, and unto the Lamb forever and ever." To those who have loved their pets and lost them, this portion of the revelation of John is comforting. Even the animals have obeyed God's laws, filled the measure of their creation, and will receive their exaltation. This principle was taught by Brigham Young (see *Journal of Discourses,* Vol. 8, p. 191), and the subject is treated by Hugh Nibley in his essay "Subduing the Earth" (*Brigham Counsels the Saints,* pp. 323). Animals receive a high and glorious reward. Also around this throne with the beasts and the elders, is the voices of angels, numbered as "ten thousand times ten thousand, and thousands and thousands" (Revelation 5:11).

This knowledge of the place God reserves for his creatures should lead all to examine their attitudes and actions toward them. Those who hope to live in a celestial environment in the life to come must now treat animals in a manner which will allow them to be comfortable with each other in that sphere. No wonder Proverbs states that "a righteous man regardeth the life of his beast" (Proverbs 12:10). The Lord gave Adam instruction for his stewardship over the animal kingdom. Dominion over the beasts, and a covering made of skins, were part of that instruction. The Word of Wisdom also teaches the proper use of the flesh of beasts:

> Yea, flesh also of beasts and of the fowls of the air, I, the Lord, have ordained for the use of man with thanksgiving; nevertheless they are to be used sparingly;
>
> And it is pleasing unto me that they should not be used, only in times of winter, or of cold, or famine.
>
> (D & C 89:12-13)

Eventually, perfect peace and safety will be established on the earth. This will extend by covenant to include all creatures:

> And in that day will I make a covenant for them with the beasts of the field, and with the fowls of heaven, and with the creeping things of the ground: and I will break the bow and the sword and the battle out of the earth, and will make them to lie down safely.
>
> (Hosea 2:18)

The Salvation of Men

In the first verse of chapter 5, John starts to describe a sealed book. Again, added information comes from the revelations of the Doctrine and Covenants:

> Q. What are we to understand by the book which John saw, which was sealed on the back with seven seals?
>
> A. We are to understand that it contains the revealed will, mysteries, and the works of God; the hidden things of his economy concerning this earth during the seven thousand years of its continuance, or its temporal existence.
>
> (D & C 77:6)

In the first five verses of chapter 5, the importance of Christ's work among the children of men is brought to attention. Only Christ is able to make the seven thousand years of the earth's history have meaning. Like a book that no one could open, the entire world history would be wasted without Christ. The reference to Christ as the Root of David refers to the eleventh chapter of Isaiah, which describes the Millennium, where he will be an ensign to the people in the latter days. Christ reveals his will, works his mysteries, and does much that is hidden from the world to save the souls of men, the beasts, and even the earth itself.

Each and every person who has ever lived, or will live, will have a wonderful story to tell about how Christ has personally and individually made his or her life worth living. The blessings of having an earth on which to dwell, the free gift of grace to overcome death, and the opportunity for exaltation are all personal gifts from the Savior. John finishes his account of his Gospel with this quote:

> And there are also many other things which Jesus did, the which if they should be written every one, I suppose that even the world itself

could not contain the books that should be written. Amen.

(John 21:25)

All who have a testimony can attest to their faith in Christ's love and concern for them. John's writing bears sacred witness to the reality of the atonement and mission of Jesus Christ, and instills a longing for the day when many will be worthy to have their faith made into a perfect knowledge. While serving as a missionary in Georgia, the author was told a story by a woman that illustrates the Savior's presence to individuals. She told of a concern she had as a young Primary-aged child. She was beginning to realize just how many children there are in the world, and wondered how Christ could actually know, love and be concerned about her personally. With a very troubled spirit, she prayed fervently. She received an answer in the form of an actual visitation from a being who radiated love. She wanted to be close to this personage. She crawled into his arms, knowing that she was personally, completely, and overwhelmingly loved. She woke up curled into a warm ball, secure in the divine knowledge that Christ was her personal, loving Savior.

6
The Earth's First 6,000 Years

Revelation 6-9 presents a whirlwind abbreviated history of the earth. D & C 77:7 clarifies that each seal is 1,000 years of the earth's temporal existence. Each 1,000 period is a dispensation, and also one day, according to the reckoning of time on the planet Kolob (Abraham 3:4). Each brief description highlights the most significant experience of that period:

Seal Number 1

Verse 2

John describes a white horse; a good representation of a pure and virgin earth, all new. A man wearing a crown sits upon the horse; Michael comes to earth from a premortal position of glory and is given dominion over the earth, much as a careful owner has over his steed. The man goes forth conquering and to conquer. What better imagery could there be of the man Adam and his posterity?

> And God blessed them, and God said unto them, Be fruitful, and multiply, and replenish the earth, and subdue it: and have dominion over the fish of the sea, and over the fowl of the air, and over every living thing that moveth upon the earth.
>
> (Genesis 1:28)

Seal Number 2

Verse 4

The horse is now red, for the earth is covered with bloodshed. Power is given him that sat thereon to take peace from the earth, that men should kill one another. The rider is wielding a great sword.

> And God said unto Noah, The end of all flesh is come before me; for the earth is filled with violence through them; and, behold, I will

destroy them with the earth.

(Genesis 6:13)

Seal Number 3

Verses 5-7

The horse is now black. The light of Christ has been rejected. This is the third thousand years. Sitting upon the horse with a pair of balances in his hand, this rider signifies the judgment that is brought upon the earth. This period was a dark age in earth's history. Abraham had to flee a land while the righteous were sacrificed to heathen gods (Abraham 1:5-7). Several tremendous famines are mentioned in which food was carefully weighed in the balance, and a day's wages, a penny (Matthew 20:2), would only purchase a day's supply of food. During one of these famines, long-term food storage, kept in Egypt under the direction of Joseph, provided the temporal salvation for the house of Israel and many others. The oil and wine being preserved could symbolize enough of the fruit of the earth that mankind does not utterly perish. (See *Doctrinal New Testament Commentary,* Vol III, p. 486.)

Seal Number 4

Verse 8

The earth is represented as a pale horse; and the rider "that sat upon him was Death, and Hell followed with him." This is the time of the great conquests: Assyria, Babylon, Greece and Rome. These great conquests were possible because of the wickedness that prevailed among the people, so naturally, when death came it was followed by hell. The horse is pale because the earth cannot bring forth its strength when a fourth part of the earth is overcome by the sword. The famine that accompanied these great conquests must have been horrendous, as soldiers burned and plundered, and women and children were left to plant and harvest. By a review of history one can see that the real wickedness of the time is demonstrated by the fact that no despotic leader can act on his own. He has to corrupt a whole people, who are then in virtual bondage themselves. Their vision becomes blurred, so that they see nothing beyond the opportunity to hold someone else down, grind their face, and make their lot worse than their own. The people who are subdued in these conquests think so little of themselves and their posterity as to allow someone to take that which is most precious, even their personal liberty. No people will ever remain in bondage when they develop the Christ-like virtue of lifting up those who are in a lower condition. When this is the case, whole societies change overnight. Among such a people, the Spirit of Christ would be pleased to dwell, and no external force would ever overcome them. They could say: "They that be with us are more than they that be with them" (2 Kings 6:16).

Seal Number 5

Verses 9-11

The fifth seal moves on to the time of Christ. It is fitting that the first image mentioned is that of an altar, representing the time of the great and last sacrifice. The law of sacrifice was taught that the ancients might look forward to Christ. His blood was spilt upon that altar to the fulfilling of the eternal law of sacrifice. Beneath the altar are the souls of those who were slain for the Word of God, which is another name for Christ, and the testimony which they held. The law of sacrifice embodies the principle that those who are willing to trade their all for a covenant promise, to them will God give his all. The price and the reward are the same for everyone. In God's infinite justice and mercy, the sacrifice exacted of each person is according to each person's ability to pay, and yet everyone pays exactly the same price; all he requires is their all.

Understanding the Atonement

It is equally valuable to look back to this ancient law to help understand the Lord's sacrifice. In Alma 7:7 the Lord teaches that of all the things to come, one is of more importance than all the rest: the Redeemer cometh among his people. How did the law of sacrifice operate? It was an introduction to the law of mercy, and a companion to the law of justice. Suppose someone had committed a sin, even a terrible sin, such as adultery. He or she would feel the loss of God's spirit, because the Lord's spirit cannot abide in impure tabernacles. The sinner would go to the priest and confess, saying, "I am guilty of a terrible offense, and feel a need to be reconciled with God, that I may once again enjoy his spirit." The priest would open the "law" and show that the penalty for adultery is death. The sinner might be asked if he wishes to pay the price for his sin. Most assuredly, the sinner would seek by any means to have claim on the mercy of the Lord.

The criminal justice system of the United States perpetuates a powerful image: a woman stands blindfolded; in one hand is a set of balances; in the other is a sword, the sword of justice. The law of justice states that there must be a payment for transgression. People always want the criminal brought to justice, but now, when they are the ones who stands condemned, oh, how they desire mercy.

The priest, who has been called by the Lord, would look at the sinner, his situation, and his sin. This grievous sin requires a significant sacrifice. The priest might admonish the sinner to bring in his best bull. He would do whatever it takes to get a spotless bull and bring it before a priest, who is the ritual slaughterer and killer of the proxy for guilt. He would lay his hands upon the bull and give the bull the sinner's name. Representing the sinner, the bull now carries his sin. The bull is then sacrificed. Its body is thrown into the flames and consumed. Some of the bull's blood is mingled with the blood of other sacrifices, and saved for the *hatat,* or ritual sprinkling on the day of Yom Kippur, which is the Day of Atonement. On this day the priest would fill the Holy of Holies with the smoke of incense. This is so that as he enters the presence of the Lord, he will not see the Lord and be slain. The blood of the sacrifices is sprinkled seven times on the veil, and then on the ark of the covenant, a portable throne of God called the mercy seat. This sprinkling of blood seven times has significance in studying the revelation of John, learning that it was Christ who gives meaning to the seven seals, or periods of the earth's temporal existence.

If the sacrifice is acceptable to the Lord, then the Lord will remain with his people, and there is an atonement, or "At-One-Ment." God and his people are at one.

Conditions for Blessings of the Atonement

This ancient law of sacrifice was a type; but it must be remembered that it was only a type. The atonement of Jesus Christ is accepted by covenant. Jesus Christ becomes your proxy, taking upon himself your name and burden. He, who is without guilt, becomes guilty for you. He takes upon himself your sins, your fallen nature, your infirmities, sickness, disease, and all imperfections. He, in your place, suffers, bleeds, and is killed for you.

> For behold, I, God, have suffered these things for all, that they might not suffer if they would repent;

> But if they would not repent they must suffer even as I;
>
> Which suffering caused myself, even God, the greatest of all, to tremble because of pain, and to bleed at every pore, and to suffer both body and spirit—and would that I might not drink the bitter cup, and shrink—
>
> Nevertheless, glory be to the Father, and I partook and finished my preparations unto the children of men.
>
> (D & C 19:16-19)

One accepts this covenant by acts of faith. He believes in Christ. This leads him to seek those who can trace their authority from Christ. The Lord has taught that one must repent and forsake his sins. By this, he is worthy to be baptized. The old person dies and is buried in the waters of baptism. In the name of the Father, the Son, and the Holy Ghost, a new person comes forth, born again, out of the water. In this cleansed condition, he is worthy to be confirmed, to take upon him the name of Christ, and receive the Holy Ghost as a guide and companion. When he takes upon himself the name of Christ, he becomes Christ's proxy. He seeks to live as Christ would live. He covenants that he is willing to give his all, and enter the strait and narrow path that leads to becoming like Christ.

Christ is the proxy in the role of Savior, and his followers are his proxy in the role of building his kingdom. One dictionary definition of proxy is: an ally or confederate who can be relied upon to speak or act in one's behalf. This definition fits with the understanding of the covenants renewed upon partaking of the sacrament. Alma 34:10 states:

> For it is expedient that there should be a great and last sacrifice; yea, not a sacrifice of man, neither of beast, neither of any manner of fowl; for it shall not be a human sacrifice; but it must be an infinite and eternal sacrifice.

Since Christ, by his nature, is infinite and eternal, only he could offer an infinite and eternal sacrifice. Christ's infinite goodness and sacrifice literally cover mankind's sins so that all who wish may enter the eternities with Christ, even before achieving perfection. By word and example, Christ teaches how to live the covenant. The Sermon on the Mount contains these teachings. The Holy Ghost becomes a personal guide. Through the partaking of the sacrament, these covenants are renewed.

Last, there is a great key involved with how the laws of mercy and justice apply:

Blessed are the merciful: for they shall obtain mercy.

(Matthew 5:7)

Judge not, that ye be not judged.
For with what judgment ye judge, ye shall be judged: and with what measure ye mete, it shall be measured to you again.

(Matthew 7:1, 2)

Sacrifice Required of the Lord

The fifth seal teaches about sacrifice. The author has always been amazed that men are willing to spend a lifetime accumulating a few pieces of earthly gold. In the eternal world, such wealth is simply dross, nothing but celestial asphalt. An interesting fact was discovered during studies done to measure the intelligence of animals. The more intelligent the animal, the longer it can delay gratification. The more intelligent creatures grasp the concept of trading a little now for a lot later on. So it is with mankind. Will a person buy or trade with Christ the riches of eternity for the little he possess in the here and now? Many were Christian martyrs (verses 9-10) during the fifth seal, and counted even their own lives as a small price to pay. In verse 11, white robes were given to every one of them. They enter into the rest of the Lord. They are told that yet others of their brethren will be killed as they were.

From the *Sixth Lecture on Faith,* Joseph Smith teaches, "Let us here observe that a religion that does not require the sacrifice of all things never has power sufficient to produce the faith necessary unto life and salvation." Further on he states, "It is in vain for persons to fancy to themselves that they are heirs with those, or can be heirs with them who have offered their all in sacrifice and by this means obtained faith in God and favor with him so as to obtain eternal life unless they in like manner offer unto him the same sacrifice and through that offering obtain the knowledge that they are accepted of him."

Seal Number 6

Verses 12-17

Pay particular attention: This is the present day! It is ushered in by a great earthquake. The aftermath of the earthquake could also explain the other signs in verses 12 and 13. As in all recorded major modern earthquakes, the smoke of many fires and the dust of the earthquake would give a filtered view of the sun, as though looking through a sackcloth. These airborne particles would also give the moon a reddish glow. The traumatic movement of the earth makes it seem as if the stars are moving. John compares it to a fig tree in winter, shaken by a mighty wind. Imagine the bare branches like arms hurling the remaining figs, as a hard ball flies from a pitcher's arm. So are the stars cast from view.

To understand verse 14, it is essential to look to the Joseph Smith Translation. The word "departed" needs to be replaced with "opened": "the heavens opened." The earth is actually moving into a new orbit, from a telestial to a terrestrial, to ready itself for the coming of its king. If the earth is to have a new heaven, it must be physically moved to achieve this (Isaiah 65:17, 66:22; 2 Peter 3:13; Revelation 21:1). The trauma on earth continues as every mountain and island is moved out of its place. The realization of what is happening dawns on kings, great men, rich men, captains, mighty men, bond men, and free men as they hide themselves, hoping to avoid their call to see the face of Christ and face his wrath. The chapter ends with a question, "Who shall be able to stand?" The question all should ask themselves is, "Shall I be able to stand?"

7
Tribulation and the Sixth Seal

The Holding of Four Winds

Verse 1 describes the holding of the four winds by four angels standing on the four corners of the earth. This event is commented upon in D & C 77:8:

> Q. What are we to understand by the four angels, spoken of in the 7th chapter and 1st verse of Revelation?
>
> A. We are to understand that they are four angels sent forth from God, to whom is given power over the four parts of the earth, to save life and to destroy; these are they who have the everlasting gospel to commit to every nation, kindred, tongue, and people; having power to shut up the heavens, to seal up unto life, or to cast down to the regions of darkness.

This scripture is then cross-referenced to D & C 133:7-8 and Joseph Smith Matthew 1:37, where it is shown that the four winds are specifically tied to the work of gathering the elect. (See also Moses 7:61, 62 where the same event is described. Here the metaphor for gathering is a flood combining righteousness from heaven with truth out of the earth.) In John 3:8, being born of the spirit is related to, as "the wind bloweth." The question one must ask is, "Why is this wind withheld, and how does this event relate to the sealing of the one hundred and forty-four thousand, and the hurting of the earth and sea that is held off until this sealing is accomplished?" The Lord has taught that the fullness of his gospel will be brought from the gentiles before it goes again unto the House of Israel (D & C 14:10; 19:27; 90:9; 107:33, 97). If the wind has to do with the spirit and the gathering of the elect, then this holding of the wind might be referring to a calling back of the missionaries prior to their return with the greater endowed power which may be necessary to do the work then required in a very troubled world. Brigham Young may have been referring to this time when he made this statement:

> When the testimony of the Elders ceases to be given, and the Lord says to them, "Come home; I will now preach my own sermons to the

nations of the earth," all that is now known can scarcely be called a preface to the sermon that will be preached with fire and sword, tempests, earthquakes, hail, rain, thunders and lightnings, and fearful destruction.
(Journal of Discourses, Vol 8, p. 123)

The Sealing of 144,000

Another angel then ascends from the east having the seal of the living God. This is also clarified from D & C 77:9:

> Q. What are we to understand by the angel ascending from the east, Revelation 7th chapter and 2nd verse?
> A. We are to understand that the angel ascending from the east is he to whom is given the seal of the living God over the twelve tribes of Israel; wherefore, he crieth unto the four angels having the everlasting gospel, saying: Hurt not the earth, neither the sea, nor the trees, till we have sealed the servants of our God in their foreheads. And, if you will receive it, this is Elias which was to come to gather together the tribes of Israel and restore all things.

This sealing of the 144,000 must include those who are yet living, because the destruction on earth is postponed until this work is done. One hundred forty-four thousand special emissaries are sealed, twelve thousand out of each tribe. Today's missionaries are sent out only after they receive their temple endowment. This endowment gives special knowledge and power to those thus endowed to better able them to fulfill their missions. This sealing signifies an even greater endowment as the 144,000 special witnesses go forth to accomplish their last mission. They are sealed "to administer the everlasting gospel . . . and to bring as many as will come to the church of the Firstborn" (D & C 77:11). This seal is not a visible mark, but it "signifies sealing the blessing upon their heads." What is this blessing? "The new and everlasting covenant, thereby making their calling and election sure" *(History of the Church,* Vol. 5; p. 530). Orson Pratt explained why it was critical that this sealing, or blessing, be given before the angels loosed the four winds:

> When the Temple is built the sons of the two Priesthoods . . . will enter into the Temple . . . and all of them who are pure in heart will behold the face of the Lord and that too before he comes in his glory in the clouds of heaven, for he will suddenly come to his Temple, and

he will purify the sons of Moses and of Aaron, until they shall be prepared to offer in that temple an offering that shall be acceptable in the sight of the Lord. In doing this, he will purify not only the minds of the Priesthood in that Temple, but he will purify their bodies until they shall be quickened, and renewed and strengthened, and they will be partially changed, not to immortality, but changed in part that they can be filled with the power of God, and they can stand in the presence of Jesus, and behold his face in the midst of that Temple.

This will prepare them for further ministrations among the nations of the earth—it will prepare them to go forth in the days of tribulation and vengeance upon the nations of the wicked, when God will smite them with pestilence, plague, and earthquake, such as former generations never knew. Then the servants of God will need to be armed with the power of God, they will need to have that sealing blessing pronounced upon their foreheads that they can stand forth in the midst of these desolations and plagues and not be overcome by them. When John the Revelator describes this scene he says he saw four angels sent forth, ready to hold the four winds that should blow from the four quarters of heaven. Another angel ascended from the east and cried to the four angels, and said, "Smite not the earth now, but wait a little while." "How long?" "Until the servant of our God are sealed in their foreheads." What for? To prepare them to stand forth in the midst of these desolations and plagues, and not be overcome. When they are prepared, when they have received a renewal of their bodies in the Lord's temple, and have been filled with the Holy Ghost and purified as gold and silver in a furnace of fire, then they will be prepared to stand before the nations of the earth and preach glad tidings of salvation in the midst of judgments that are to come like a whirlwind upon the wicked.

(Journal of Discourses, 15:365-66.
See Malachi 3:1-4; D & C 128:24)

The position forwarded by a religious sect of this day, that these one hundred forty-four thousand are the only ones who will be heirs of salvation, is not upheld by the scriptures (Revelation 7:9). The Prophet Joseph Smith also taught, "There will be 144,000 saviors on Mount Zion, and with them an innumerable host that no man can number. Oh! I beseech you to go forward, go forward and make your calling and your election sure; and if any man preach any other Gospel than that which I have preached, he shall be cursed." (*History of the Church,* Vol. 6, p. 365.)

The Blessings of Great Tribulation

In viewing this happy and numerous host before the Lamb, the most important question is, "What did they do, or how did they get there?" The answer is found in verse 14: "These are they that came out of great tribulation!"

The sorrows and troubles of life are necessary, a gift which helps one to be sufficiently humble, that the righteous can, as verse 14 states, "wash our robes and make them white in the blood of the Lamb." This is a beautiful metaphor, one that embodies the awe-inspiring miracle of the atonement. Bloodstains on clothing are the most difficult stains to remove. Yet the Lord promises that those who symbolically submerge their earth-stained garments in Christ's atoning blood will come up spotless, pure, and white. Christ's blood is the symbol of his condescension to save this world. Through Christ's blood all can become sanctified, accept the living waters of his love, and be spiritually cleansed. Having overcome the world through Christ, such are worthy of the promises given in Revelation 7:16-17.

Before leaving the sixth seal, it is noteworthy to discuss what it means to "come out of tribulation." In Moses 7:61, the Lord tells Moses that before the day comes that the earth will rest, the heavens will be darkened and shake, and also the earth will shake, and "great tribulations shall be among the children of men, but my people will I preserve." In Matthew 24:37, the Savior teaches, "As the days of Noah were, so shall also the coming of the Son of man be." Noah's day is usually thought of as a time when all men delighted in wickedness, but that is not the only hallmark of his day. These writings in the Book of Moses teach that this was also a time when the righteous came forth *out of great tribulation* to establish Zion. The author believes that the account of Enoch is given because it typifies the last days, the time and the work in which the righteous will be involved. It is well worth studing this in connection with the Revelation of John.

Likening Enoch to the Last Days

The account of Enoch is fittingly found in the Pearl of Great Price, in Moses 6. The first thing Moses would have known is that a book of remembrance was being kept. Moses 6:5 states that it was recorded in the language of Adam, and it was given to as many as who called upon God to write by the spirit of inspiration. These were scriptures. Moses 6:6 describes the vital function they served: these righteous saints taught their children to read and write with them, for their language was pure and undefiled. It is interesting to note that until not very long ago, the Bible was the number-one textbook used in the schools in America, and public schools were put forth as a great and grand plan whereby everyone could learn to read the Bible.

By contrast, in verse 15 Moses reveals the general state of the earth:

> And the children of men were numerous upon all the face of the land. And in those days Satan had great dominion among men, and raged in their hearts; and from thenceforth came wars and bloodshed; and a man's hand was against his own brother, in administering death, because of secret works, seeking for power.
>
> (Moses 6:15)

Why was this happening? "Because of secret works, seeking for power." The wickedness was such that verse 17 tells that it was necessary that there be an exodus. The righteous are lead to a land of promise called Canaan. The great prophet Enoch is introduced, as he hears the voice of the Lord calling him on a mission:

> Enoch, my son, prophesy unto this people, and say unto them— Repent, for thus saith the Lord: I am angry with this people, and my fierce anger is kindled against them; for their hearts have waxed hard, and their ears are dull of hearing, and their eyes can not see afar off."
>
> (Moses 6:27)

The people are to be rebuked because they have a spiritual hardening of the arteries, hearing loss, and near-sightedness. Also, in verse 28, the Lord again says they "have denied me, and have sought their own counsels in the dark; and in their own abominations have they devised murder, and have not kept the commandments."

Enoch's reply to the Lord's call comes as a lament: "Why is it that I have found favor in thy sight, and am but a lad, and all the people hate me; for I am slow of speech; wherefore am I thy servant?" It seems that even the prophets are given thorns in the flesh. As for being but a lad, verse 25 teaches that Enoch is 65 years old. All things are relative, for in his day, prophets lived to be nearly a thousand years old!

Enoch begins his mission by receiving a covenant promise:

> And the Lord said unto Enoch: Go forth and do as I have commanded thee, and no man shall pierce thee. Open thy mouth, and it shall be

filled, and I will give unto thee utterance, for all flesh is in my hands, and I will do as seemeth me good.

(Moses 6:32)

He begins to fulfill his part of the covenant by going forth and doing as the Lord commands. He is given a promise of divine protection, and is assured that, despite his slow speech, the Holy Ghost will open his mouth that he will be able to speak. The verse ends with this reminder: "All flesh is in my hands, and I will do as seemeth me good." In spite of the wickedness of the world, the Lord is running the show.

Lessons from Enoch's Teaching

As missionaries, many learn how easy it is to offend people, but Enoch was a master. Verse 38 states that Enoch was able to offend *all* men. The crowds gather to see a "strange thing in the land; a wild man hath come among us." Enoch teaches the people that the way they are living is not acceptable, and that there is a different, better way to live. There is yet a land of righteousness upon the earth. In this land the people have prophets, even Adam, the first of all (Moses 6:45), and a pattern given by the finger of God in their book of remembrance.

What was it that Enoch taught that had such a profound influence on his people? His teachings are found in verses 52-68: faith, repentance, baptism, and receiving the Holy Ghost. "For by the water ye keep the commandments; by the Spirit ye are justified, and by the blood ye are sanctified" (Moses 6:60). Christ's followers keep the commandments by being baptized. They receive the Holy Ghost and are justified. They accept the atonement and are sanctified. Then they are promised the peaceable things of immortal glory (verse 61). In a day of great wickedness, war, and bloodshed, this is a profound promise. Through obedience to the first four principles and ordinances of the gospel, the people followed Enoch and were led to become the people of God!

After completing the draft for this book, the author kept having a feeling that he was leaving something out of this section. After returning to the scriptures, he found that there was more. It wasn't just what was taught to the people, but it was taught in a specific way. Since this is stated twice in Moses 6:57-58, it should not be overlooked: *Parents were to learn the gospel from the prophet and then teach it to their children.*

Times of greatest learning come through teaching. It has also been observed that if one cannot explain a concept so that a child can understand it, he really does not understand it himself. The humblest parents who call upon the Lord and are willing to take their children's hands, saying, "Let's learn together," will be more effective teachers to those children than the most sophisticated and educated hireling that could be obtained.

The Lord Protects His People

Moses 7:13 describes the divine defense system that protected the people of Enoch:

> And their enemies came to battle against them; and he spake the word of the Lord, and the earth trembled, and the mountains fled, even according to his command; and the rivers of water were turned out of their course; and the roar of the lions was heard out of the wilderness; and all nations feared greatly, so powerful was the word of Enoch, and so great was the power of the language which God had given him.
> (Moses 7:13)

The nature of a great division is clarified in verse 16: "And from that time forth there were wars and bloodshed among them; but the Lord came and dwelt with his people, and they dwelt in righteousness." Perhaps the world's wicked state allowed Enoch's people to see more clearly the contrast in the plan the Lord had set forth. "And the Lord called his people Zion, because they were of one heart and one mind, and dwelt in righteousness; and there was no poor among them" (7:18). This is the description of a people worthy to be called *out of great tribulation* to be the Lord's people.

Enoch was also privileged to see the great vision: "And it came to pass that the Lord showed unto Enoch all the inhabitants of the earth" (7:21). He also witnessed the doings of Satan: "And he beheld Satan; and he had a great chain in his hand, and it veiled the whole face of the earth with darkness; and he looked up and laughed, and his angels rejoiced" (7:26). This chain is a symbol of bondage, which occurs not only among nations, but among individuals whenever freedom is lost, whether to enslaving habits, debts, captivity or sin.

In the next verse, Enoch beholds angels descending out of heaven, bearing testimony of the Father and Son: "and the Holy Ghost fell upon many, and they were caught up by the powers of heaven into Zion." How many children have loved the story of Noah and the Ark? Beautiful animals, from aardvark and antelope to yak and zebra, boarded the ark at Noah's authoritative call. Many of these same children close their picture books and wonder how everyone could be so wicked that the Lord would destroy them all, including the little children and tiny babies. Latter-day Saint children should be taught this precious pearl of great price: the righteous were caught up to heaven before the Lord allowed the floodwater to rise and destroy the wicked! Enoch witnessed that the God of heaven looked upon the residue of the people and wept. They must have been incredibly wicked for the Lord, who is perfect and from eternity to eternity, to cry over their demise. Verse 32 tells the reason: "The Lord said unto Enoch: behold these thy brethren; they are the workmanship of mine own hands, and I gave unto them their knowledge, in the day I created them; and in the Garden of Eden, gave I unto man his agency" (Moses 7:32).

The extent of the people's wickedness at the time of Enoch and Noah is laid forth in verse 36: "Wherefore, I can stretch forth mine hands and hold all the creations which I have made; and mine eye can pierce them also, and among all the workmanship of mine hands there has not been so great wickedness as among thy brethren." Enoch opened his heart to the pain that comes with understanding: "Enoch knew, and looked upon their wickedness, and their misery, and wept and stretched forth his arms, and his heart swelled wide as eternity; and his bowels yearned; and all eternity shook" (7:41). After this taste of godly sorrow, Enoch refused to be comforted, but the Lord had yet other lessons to teach him. Enoch then saw the day of the coming of the Son of Man. Enoch looked upon the earth and heard a voice from the bowels of the earth saying, "Wo, wo is me, the mother of men; I am pained, I am weary, because of the wickedness of my children. When shall I rest, and be cleansed from all the filthiness which has gone forth out of me? When will my Creator sanctify me, that I may rest, and righteousness for a season abide upon my face?" (7:48). When Enoch heard the earth mourn, he wept, and cried unto the Lord, saying: "O Lord, wilt thou not have compassion upon the earth? Wilt thou not bless the children of Noah?" (7:49). He saw that the earth will rest, but before it does there will be a day of great tribulation.

The Lord promises that he will preserve his people (7:61). In the next verse, the Lord promises that in these latter days, "righteousness and truth will

I cause to sweep the earth as with a flood, to gather out mine elect from the four quarters of the earth, unto a place which I shall prepare, an Holy City, that my people may gird up their loins, and be looking forth for the time of my coming; for there shall be my tabernacle, and it shall be called Zion, a New Jerusalem." Enoch's Zion will yet be joined with the righteous on the earth. The fulfillment of Noah's covenant comes in these latter days! By building Zion on earth, the saints look up. The Heavenly Zion, by returning, looks down, until the two, in joy, are reunited. Verse 63 gives to modern saints this beautiful description of that anticipated reunion: "We will fall upon their necks, and they shall fall upon our necks, and we will kiss each other." Last, the earth is promised its thousand years of rest.

The tribulation of the wicked is contrasted with the fullness of joy and redemption received by the righteous: "And Enoch and all his people walked with God, and he dwelt in the midst of Zion. And it came to pass that Zion was not, for God received it up into his own bosom; and from thence went forth the saying, ZION IS FLED" (7:69).

It is not only possible, but it actually has been accomplished in times past, for a people in righteousness to be brought out and separated from the tribulations, suffering, and vengeance of God poured out upon the wicked. The strait and narrow path is the only shortcut. When the Savior reveals that this day is as the days of Noah, it is both *a curse and blessing*.

8
The Seven Latter-day Plagues

The Opening of the Seventh Seal

Christ has not yet come to the world in general. Before the earth is ready for its sabbath rest and worship, preparation and cleansing are still needed. The opening of this seal brings one-half hour of silence in the heavens. There has been much speculation as to the meaning of this period of silence in heaven. Two additional scriptures in the Doctrine and Covenants mention such an event or events:

> For all flesh is corrupted before me; and the powers of darkness prevail upon the earth, among the children of men, in the presence of all the hosts of heaven—
> Which causeth *silence* to reign, and all eternity is pained, and the angels are waiting the great command to reap down the earth, to gather the tares that they may be burned; and, behold, the enemy is combined.
> And now I show unto you a mystery, a thing which is had in secret chambers, to bring to pass even your destruction in process of time, and ye knew it not;
> (D & C 38:11-13)

> And immediately there shall appear a great sign in heaven, and all people shall see it together.
> And another angel shall sound his trump, saying: That great church, the mother of abominations, that made all nations drink of the wine of the wrath of her fornication, that persecuteth the saints of God, that shed their blood—she who sitteth upon many waters, and upon the islands of the sea—behold, she is the tares of the earth; she is bound in bundles; her bands are made strong, no man can loose them; therefore, she is ready to be burned. And he shall sound his trump both long and loud, and all nations shall hear it.
> And there shall be *silence in heaven for the space of half an hour;* and immediately after shall the curtain of heaven be unfolded, as a scroll is unfolded after it is rolled up, and the face of the Lord shall be unveiled.
> (D & C 88:93-95)

In both instances the silence is tied to a period of earthly wickedness. Specifically mentioned is the fact that the enemy, the tares of the earth, the great whore, is combined and ready to be burned. Other than these three scriptures, there is very little to help determine what this half hour of silence means. Is it literal, or is there some other meaning? Could this be a period where the voice of earthly Satanic institutions is so overwhelming that only a small percentage of the earth's population are hearing the still small voice, and truly heeding Christ's message?

One Theory About Heaven's Silence

Based on its far-reaching impact, one other interesting possible interpretation is that the half hour of silence in heaven might be tied to the time that God should be hearing prayer that is now missing or silent from public affairs, as mandated by law. An excellent treatment of the subject is found in the book *America, to Pray or Not to Pray,* a statistical look at what happened when religious principles were separated from public affairs (David Barton). Mr. Barton notes that on June 25, 1962, the Supreme Court first struck down school prayer by prohibiting students from using this simple invocation:

> "Almighty God, we acknowledge our dependence upon thee, and beg thy blessing upon us, our parents, our teachers, and our country."

Following this case, the court began methodically expelling other religious principles. The effects have been most evident. Using dramatic graphs, charts, and tables, 1963 is proved to be a most important pivotal year, negatively, in U.S. history. This book looks at birth rates and pregnancies to unwed girls, gonorrhea, premarital sexual activity, teens who are sexually active, decrease in male and female virgins on college campuses, students attitudes towards rape, divorce rates, single-parent households, unmarried couples living together, adultery, SAT scores looked at as total, verbal, math, and also significant points, ACT scores, school dropouts, international testing, multifactor productivity on farms and private business, cases of sexually transmitted disease, alcohol consumption per capita, and reported child abuse. This book also looks at other related factors, and even shows that the same negative statistics do not carry over to the private Christian schools. The statistics are shown in a manner that the reader can clearly see that the negative growth is far greater than would be projected from population growth and past history.

One cannot ignore God with impunity. David O. McKay stated, "By making that unconstitutional, the Supreme Court of the United States severs the connecting cord between the public schools of the United States, and the source of divine intelligence, the Creator, Himself . . . Evidently, the Supreme Court misinterprets the true meaning of the First Amendment, and now are leading a Christian nation down the road to atheism." (*Prophets, Principles, and National Survival,* pp. 185-188). To understand what influence the Supreme Court was operating under when it made such a decision, 2 Nephi 32:8 reveals, " . . . for the evil spirit teacheth not a man to pray, but teacheth him that he must not pray."

Prophecy of Seven Great Plagues

Significantly, the reference to this half hour of silence in Revelation proceeds John's description of the seven great plagues of the last days. Some have put forth the thought that perhaps the half hour of silence may be using the Lord's time frame (1,000 years to a day, or just short of 21 years). The event described in D & C 88 is tied to signs in heaven that all people shall hear and see together, and also the starting of the events of Christ's millennial reign. This silence ends when the seven angels which stood before God are given seven trumpets to herald in the earth's Sabbath day before the Lord comes again.

This is brought to light by the answer to Joseph Smith's questions in D & C 77:12:

> Q. What are we to understand by the sounding of the trumpets, mentioned in the 8th chapter of Revelation?
>
> A. We are to understand that as God made the world in six days, and on the seventh day he finished his work, and sanctified it, and also formed man out of the dust of the earth, even so, in the beginning of the seventh thousand years will the Lord God sanctify the earth, and complete the salvation of man, and judge all things, and shall redeem all things, except that which he hath not put into his power, when he shall have sealed all things, unto the end of all things; and the sounding of the trumpets of the seven angels are the preparing and finishing of his work, in the beginning of the seventh thousand years—the preparing of the way before the time of his coming.
>
> (D & C 77:12)

John seemed to be describing the great council at Adam-ondi-Ahman:

> Spring Hill is named by the Lord Adam-ondi-Ahman, because, said he, it is the place where Adam shall come to visit his people, or the Ancient of Days shall sit, as spoken of by Daniel the prophet.
>
> (D & C 116)

The seven angels are the prophets of all the dispensations, including Christ, who gather there for a special conference. This conference is a coming of Christ, but it is not to the world generally, and most of the world will be unaware. At this conference the keys of all dispensations are present, an accounting is given, and the seven trumpets are given to Christ, who is the Lord of the earth's sabbath or millennium.

In verse 3, an angel holds much incense to be offered with the prayers of all the saints upon the altar before the throne. The altar (place of sacrifice) is mentioned in connection with the Saints (the righteous on earth) who are earnestly praying. During the fifth seal the same kind of prayers were offered upon the altar (Revelation 6:10). The saints then living were to be gathered with the dead of that era, and then were told to rest for a little season. During the seventh seal, justice, vengeance, and destruction are poured out upon the wicked without measure.

Seven great periods of destruction are now decreed. When looking at the seven plagues of the last days, one may also look for similarities with the plagues of Egypt in the days of Moses. Though the plagues themselves are quite different, the Lord's message through them may be identical. To the Lord's people the message was "Come ye out and be a separate people." To Egypt the message was "Let my people go." Many references are to the destruction being meted out on a third part. This may be a symbolic and actual cleansing of the earth of the influence and effects of Satan and the one-third of the hosts of heaven that followed him (Revelation 12:4; D & C 29:36-37).

Woes of the Seventh Seal

In the seventh seal a great earthquake is mentioned (Revelation 8:5). Many believe that there is an overlap between the sixth and seventh seals, which will be addressed in a following chapter of this book in the discussion of the time of the second coming. The ending of the sixth seal also contains a reference to a great earthquake, commonly referred to as "the big one"

(Revelation 6:12). Note that when the earthquake appears, the conference at Adam-ondi-Ahman has already occurred. This gives an event by which to set time-line bearings.

Verse 7 enters into the first of the "Woes." This destruction comes after the sounding of the angel. In chapter 9 these plagues are carried out by wicked kings, armies, and their implements of war. So what is the significance of their occurring after the sounding or the apparent approval of an angel? John may be reminding again that the whole world is in Christ's hands. Bounds are set which they cannot pass, and the Lord does use the wicked to destroy the wicked (Mormon 4:5). There are many other examples of this principle. The Savior said that Pilate had no power except what had been allowed to him (John 19:11). Ancient Israel was continually promised deliverance or destruction, not by any world conditions, the strength of their armies or the cunning of their leaders, but rather dependent on their faith, obedience, righteousness, and covenants.

The Destructions in Modern-day Terms

If these events are viewed in the context of man-made destructions, it is easy to get a clear picture of the unfolding drama. The *first angel* sounds to usher in the first "Woe." What follows is hail and fire mingled with blood. This is a pretty good description of conventional warfare, which the whole world has witnessed because of the marvel of television. John describes white streaks of the rocket and shells, followed by fires and flames of destruction mingled with blood. The author believes John is saying that the seven "Woes" will begin with a conventional war.

The second angel sounds. John uses the phrase "as it were"—he has trouble explaining what he is seeing in the language and experience of his day. He describes a great mountain, burning with fire, cast into the sea. This may be a description of the first unleashing of the weapons of mass destruction used on a limited basis in naval warfare. The human race has a history of using all of the weapons of war it amasses. Use of these weapons in naval warfare would be a logical beginning. The oceans of the earth cover a massive area, so this is truly a huge destruction when one-third part of the creatures of the sea and one-third part of all ships are destroyed. In witnessing this second "Woe," John gives a final warning to complete preparations for the next and upcoming plagues. This mapping out of the seven plagues in type and specific order may be one of the greatest blessings to temporal salvation that studying the Book of Revelation brings.

At the sounding of the *third angel* comes the falling of a great star from heaven, burning as if it were a lamp. The actual destruction of this falling star is greatly overshadowed by the contamination carried out in the waters (Revelation 8:10). The author believes this to be an actual land-based nuclear exchange. It is now known, from what happened at Chernobyl, that destruction by contamination can be far worse than actual, immediate nuclear destruction. The name of this falling star is Wormwood. Wormwood is also an herb. Metaphorically, it symbolizes the bitter calamity, or sorrow, such as would occur after the unleashing of this destruction. "Many men died of the waters because they were made bitter" (Revelation 8:11).

Wormwood—A Modern Parallel

The author believes that John was prophesying a nuclear emergency and believes there are many interesting evidences to support this claim. The name Wormwood may be a clue to the nature of this plague. As if in preliminary warning, the name *Chernobyl* in Russian can be translated as *wormwood*. The city of Chernobyl is named after the wild native plant *Chernobylnic*, a wild form of *Polyn'*. *Polyn'* is a direct translation for *wormwood* as it appears in the Russian Bible. Therefore, the most publicized incident of contamination from nuclear radiation is from a place called Wormwood!

Another interesting clue is given in D & C 112:24-25:

> Behold, vengeance cometh speedily upon the inhabitants of the earth, a day of wrath, a day of burning, a day of desolation, of weeping, of mourning, and of lamentation; and as a whirlwind it shall come upon all the face of the earth, saith the Lord.
>
> And upon my house shall it begin, and from my house shall it go forth, saith the Lord;

The first nuclear bomb was assembled and the mission was launched, or "went forth," from Wendover, Utah. Most are aware of the United States government's lack of caution as it secretly conducted nuclear testings in the Western United States. The extent of the destruction and suffering is documented in a book titled *The Day We Bombed Utah*. If it is possible for some immunity to be built by such exposure, this may prove to be a blessing for the upcoming contamination. Nevertheless, this was a gross misuse of government power.

In searching for other possible clues from wormwood, one must study it as an herb. There are numerous herb-related scriptures in the Bible. D & C 42:43 explains:

> And whosoever among you are sick, and have not faith to be healed, but believe, shall be nourished with all tenderness, with herbs and mild food, and that not by the hand of an enemy.

From the Book of Mormon, Alma also teaches:

> And there were some who died with fevers, which at some seasons of the year were very frequent in the land—but not so much so with fevers, because of the excellent qualities of the many plants and roots which God had prepared to remove the cause of diseases, to which men were subject by the nature of the climate.
>
> (Alma 46:40)

If plants, roots and herbs are especially prepared by God to remove the "cause of disease," and since the nature of this great destruction is obviously already known by God, could he be giving a clue as to a God-given remedy to counteract the plague? Significantly, in the scriptures *bitter herb* is used three times as a symbol preceding deliverance. The first event (Exodus 12:8) preceded the children of Israel's deliverance and reckoning of a new time (Exodus 12:2). The second event occurred as Christ was given bitter herb (gall and vinegar) before the crucifixion, preceding his deliverance and victory over the grave. This third event is that the earth is given the bitter herb wormwood before its victory and resurrection as a new earth, in a new time.

In looking at traditional uses for the herb *wormwood,* the following can be found:

> Wormwood: (Artemisia Absinthium) Parts used: herb, leaves.

Because of its bitter nature, ancient doctors used wormwood when they felt patients needed to suffer for their sins, thus the second part of the name, ab—Latin, *to move away from;* and sin—*transgression.* This is a powerful herb, used only in small quantities and for short periods of time. Care should be used when giving it to children. Wormwood is used for complaints of the digestive system. Interestingly, the major killer with radiation sickness is dehydration caused by fluid loss from diarrhea and vomiting. This herb is an expeller of toxins and poisons. It stimulates one of the body's major toxin-expelling systems by sweating, which relieves some of the stress on the digestive system. It has been used externally and internally to check falling hair and baldness. Baldness, scabs, and hair loss are mentioned elsewhere in the scriptures as part of the last-day plagues (Isaiah 3:16-26). The herb sounds pretty symptom-specific for radiation sickness. Wormwood is also a lovely perennial shrub, and given its reputation, a good conversation piece.

Note: Much of this information has been gleaned by the author over the years while directing the research and development department of a family-owned nutritional supplement manufacturing company. The author's favorite down-to-earth herbal reference book that covers this subject is *Today's Herbal Health,* by Louise Tenney, 1983, Provo, Utah: Woodland Books, p. 135.

Other Precautions Against the Plague

In counteracting this plague, there are some other preparations and precautions that should be made. Of course, the scriptures teach that faith and obedience to God are the primary defense against the adversary. While on the subject of a general conference talk, the late Apostle Bruce R. McConkie said, "It may be, for instance, that nothing except the power of faith and authority of the priesthood can save individuals and congregations from the atomic holocausts that surely shall be" (*Ensign,* May 1979, p. 93). Earlier, in Brother McConkie's *Doctrinal New Testament Commentary* (Vol. III, p. 499), he stated: "Most of the plagues and destructions, here announced for the early days of the seventh seal, are of such a nature that they (speculatively!) could be brought to pass in a large part through atomic warfare." Since this plague is specifically directed toward the whore "Babylon" (Revelation 17:1, 16), it would seem that a prerequisite would be the removal of Babylon from hearts, homes, and communities.

In the case of nuclear contamination, people will need protection (underground or in an isolated place) for a minimum of three weeks. Every seven days, Iodine 131 radiation drops by 50 percent. Food, water, a place of security, and above all, a plan for each family's security would be the key here. "A prudent man foreseeth the evil and hideth himself; but the simple pass on and are punished" (Proverbs 22:3).

Protections Against Nuclear Contamination

1. Adequate iodine intake. When cells are saturated with iodine, they will not pick up the radioactively contaminated Iodine 131. Kelp is the world's highest natural food source of this nutrient, but potassium iodine, because of its highly concentrated form, seems to be the source of choice in most literature.

2. Fresh sprouts, especially wheat, seem to protect on a cellular level. The author is aware of an unpublished study in which three groups of ten mice each were given a lethal dose of radiation. In group one, where nothing unusual was done, all ten mice died. In group two, where they were fed wheat sprouts, nine out of the ten lived. In group three, where the sprouts where grown under special conditions to increase their output of a special enzyme called SOD, ten out of ten lived. This information was related to the author, personally, by the head of the research department of a nutritional manufacturing company. This company does not ordinarily conduct animal studies, and did not publish this study because of the bad publicity it might generate in their market (which is largely vegetarian). The research was conducted to confirm earlier reports.

3. Fresh, green, uncontaminated alfalfa has been used successfully to counteract radiation sickness, build immunity, and promote health.

4. A clinic in the Hiroshima area used, with dynamic results, sea water therapy, both to bathe the burns and as a food supplement, following the bomb's devastation. Uncontaminated sea water is a wonderful source of trace minerals and is excellent for balancing the body's mineral system. It is interesting that the two major sources of inland sea water are found near promised lands of the latter-day: Utah's Great Salt Lake and the Dead Sea in Israel.

The sounding of the *fourth angel* brings what the author believes to be the aftermath of a nuclear exchange. The dust, smoke, and airborne particles block out a third part of the sun, moon, and stars (Revelation 8:12) for a period of time. Many on the earth at this time will have lost all hope. The feeling among the faithless and those who have no vision is to accept peace at any price. The destruction from this nuclear exchange, while great and tragic, is not the end of the world. The misinformation about the possibility of surviving this type of warfare may be deliberate. The former Soviet Union has long held the belief that a nuclear war is survivable and winnable. If a person is prepared, knowledgeable, determined, and lucky enough not to be directly around the detonation center, chances of survival are almost assured. In the days of Moses, the Lord's people were removed from Egypt;

in the last days, Egypt, epitomized by pride, sophistication, false beliefs, and material possessions, may be removed from the Lord's people. The people who are ready and prepared will come through. For those who hope that it is all over at this point, their hope is in vain, for three angels are yet to sound (Revelation 8:13).

9
Two Great World Conflicts

The *fifth angel* has now sounded, and chapter 9 begins by depicting an army as locusts coming out of the bottomless pit. This force is used to maintain a miserable, uneasy peace (the army is commanded not to kill). This has a duration of five months. One could gain some understanding of the philosophy of this group, as they were commanded not to hurt the grass of the earth, neither any green thing, neither any tree. Using a last-days perspective and taking into consideration the current power of the environmental or green movement, this prophecy does not seem absurd or unlikely. The reason given for the seizing of this power: the smoke that darkens the sun and air.

Environmentalism Used for Evil Purposes

Could the environmental movement spawn a world leader; or perhaps more realistic, could a world movement spawn an environmentalist leader? There are some last days parallels. Mikhail Gorbachev, former head of the Soviet Union, is now head of a new organization called the International Green Cross. He has been transformed from a communist/socialist to an ecological, save the planet, savior. A report from the Council of the Club of Rome, of which Gorbachev is a member, titled *The First Global Revolution,* p. 115 stated:

> In searching for a new enemy to unite us, we came up with the idea that pollution, the threat of global warming, water shortages, famine and the like would fit the bill . . . . All these dangers are caused by human intervention . . . . The real enemy, then, is humanity itself.

The smoke, destruction, and fearful state of the earth's inhabitants, caused by the previous plagues, may have conditioned the people to accept peace (this tyrant who at least is not killing them) at any price. The price in this instance is subjection to a tyrannical world leader. This uneasy peace and power is held at the expense of the people of the earth! Verse 6 reads, "And in those days shall men seek death, and shall not find it; and shall desire to die, and death shall flee from them." President Ezra Taft Benson, in his "must read" book, *An Enemy Hath Done This,* p. 172, puts it this way: "Americans have always accepted Patrick Henry's choice of 'Liberty or Death.' As a result, we now have liberty. If we should ever come to place mere survival above all else, if we should now make our national slogan 'Better Red than dead,' we shall end up Red and only wish that we were dead."

The image John gives of the means of enforcement reads like a description of helicopter gunships. He says their shape is that of locusts. They are armored like horses prepared unto battle. They have crowns like gold—perhaps the prop housing? Their hair is like women—the whirling props could give this impression. The faces are as the faces of men. To someone who didn't know the working of a helicopter, the faces of men looking out of the craft would appear as part of the creature. They have breastplates of iron. They are flying machines, and the sound of their wings is as the sound of many chariots and many horses running to battle. The rhythmic sound of the rotor blades truly does give the impression of horse's hooves on hard rock.

This force is under the direction of a king, an angel from the bottomless pit who is given the Hebrew name *Abaddon,* or in Greek, *Apollyon* (Revelation 9:11). The hope of the saints is that the torments of this plague are specifically directed toward those who do not have the seal of God in their foreheads. Twice it is stated that this plague has a limited duration of five months (Revelation 9:5, 10).

Army of 200 Million Assembled

Two more "Woes" are yet to come upon the earth (Revelation 9:12). The *sixth angel* sounds, releasing four angels that are bound in the great river Euphrates or 'bottomless pit,' as the Joseph Smith Translation reveals. These world leaders have amassed an army of two hundred million soldiers. The sounds of this battle seem to be symbols of heavy ground artillery. The power is in their mouths, issuing fire and smoke and brimstone. The battle is prepared for an enormous and short-lived destruction, lasting an hour, a day, a month, and a year, with one-third of all men left dead. The author believes that the short time frames mentioned are actual, for the numbers used are not those commonly associated with symbolism in the scriptures. There are other references to rapid, last days climactic events:

And except those days should be shortened, there should none of their flesh be saved; but for the elect's sake, according to the covenant, those days shall be shortened.

(Joseph Smith Matthew 1:20)

Chapter 10 of Isaiah outlines a type of the last-days battle. Brevity is again mentioned: "For yet a very little while, and the indignation shall cease, and mine anger in their destruction" (Isaiah 10:25).

The situation is the same as it was in the final days of the Jaredites and Nephites. In Book of Mormon history, the thirst for blood actually accelerated as the carnage increased. Revelation 9:20-21 points out that there will be no repentance here yet. Sorceries are among the sins listed. In Mormon 1:14 it is shown that the gifts of the spirit had ceased among the Nephites, but verse 19 of the same chapter shows that there were sorceries, witchcraft, and magics, and the power of the evil one was wrought upon all the face of the land. When the spirit of God withdraws, the void is filled with power from Satan.

10
John's Mission to Heirs of Salvation

In studying chapter 10 one may notice a dramatic shift in the tone of the message. Remember that John has described only six "Woes" or plagues, whereas seven were decreed. Revelation 10:7 does indicate that "in the days of the voice of the *seventh angel,* when he shall begin to sound, the mystery of God should be finished." It seems that at this point, John pauses to sharpen perspective and to teach. John sees another mighty and most glorious angel (Revelation 10:1). This angel has a book and sets his right foot upon the sea and his left foot upon the earth. There is the voice of seven thunders, which probably ties in some way with the sounding of the seven trumpets, which have already been mentioned.

Joshua, the prophet, can be used as a type of Christ at his second coming, and Jericho as a type of the world. The seven trumpets are a type of the voices of the seven angels. This interesting cross-reference or parallel is found in Joshua 6:16:

> And it came to pass at the seventh time, when the priests blew with the trumpets, Joshua said unto the people, Shout; for the LORD hath given you the city.
>
> (Joshua 6:16)

John was about to write what he had heard, but evidently it is information the world is not ready to receive. This sealed portion of John's record, which bears witness of the fullness of Christ's glory, will be received if the Lord's people are faithful (D & C 93:6, 18).

The Angel Who Ends Telestial Time

John again sees the angel standing upon the sea and the earth, his hand lifted up to heaven. This gesture signifies or brings about a situation when time is no longer (Revelation 10:6). Many assume that time will end at the close of the millennium, but this is not so, and there are two reasons why this happens at this time. Doctrine and Covenants 88:110 teaches that Satan is then bound:

> And so on, until the *seventh angel* shall sound his trump; and he shall stand forth upon the land and upon the sea, and swear in the name of him who sitteth upon the throne, that there shall be time no longer; and Satan shall be bound, that old serpent, who is called the devil, and shall not be loosed for the space of a thousand years.
>
> (D & C 88:110)

It was the fall of Adam that started time (this temporal, or temporary, existence), and it appears that when Satan is bound it will stop (*Doctrines of Salvation,* Vol. 1, pp. 80-81). It is known that when the earth enters its new orbit, it will be a new heaven and a new earth (Tenth Article of Faith; Isaiah 65:17-25; 66:22-24; D & C 101:23-31). The relationship between the heavens, the earth, and sea dictates time and the lunar calendar. This gives significance to the angel standing upon the heaven, earth, and sea. This is the end of telestial time.

This sealed part of the vision probably contains the missing seventh "Woe," the promised separation of the righteous and the final destruction of the unrepentant wicked who remain on the earth after the sixth "Woe" (Revelation 9:20-21). John does, however, give some clues. Verse 7 tells that when the voice of the seventh angel begins to sound, the mystery of God, as declared to his servants the prophets, will be finished.

John is then given a personal mission. He is told to go and take the little book which is open and in the hand of him that standeth upon the sea and upon the earth. Remember that this is the angel who signifies the end of time. Doctrine and Covenants 77:14 gives more light on the subject:

> Q. What are we to understand by the little book which was eaten by John, as mentioned in the 10th chapter of Revelation?
>
> A. We are to understand that it was a mission, and an ordinance, for him to gather the tribes of Israel; behold, this is Elias who, as it is written, must come and restore all things.
>
> (D & C 77:14)

John is told to eat the book; it will be in his mouth sweet as honey, but it will make his belly bitter. What type of a mission would be sweet in the mouth, but give a bitter belly? In pondering the possible meaning of this scripture, the word *vengeance* came very powerfully into the mind of the author. The scriptures teach that the day of the Lord's coming will be a day of vengeance (D & C 133:51). John is called to gather the tribes of Israel in the role of Elias, one who comes before and prepares the way. If John, as one still living, receives the mission to gather the twelve tribes, and this is somehow linked to the calling of twelve thousand especially endowed servants of God out of each tribe, could it be that John leads the army not only to gather the righteous, but also to destroy the wicked? The author believes it is quite possible; such a mission would definitely be bitter and sweet. This destruction, whether or not it is part of John's earthly mission, is alluded to in the parable of the wheat and the tares (D & C 101:44-62). It is known that the seventh "woe" will destroy the remaining wicked from off the face of the earth, and that the righteous will be gathered first.

Chapter 10 concludes the whirlwind-abbreviated history of the world as represented by the seven seals. It tells what has happened, and what is to happen. In verse 11, John is told that he needs to prophesy again, this time before many people, nations, and tongues, and kings. In the chapters to come, John adds details and perspective by describing these events from more than one angle.

The Time of the Second Coming

In the Lord's time frame, the coming of the Savior for the second time, to rule and reign in glory, could be minutes away, or up to an hour at the most (Abraham 3:4, 2 Peter 3:8). Some have put forth the argument that the second coming of Christ has to be in the year 2,000. This is their reasoning: seven thousand years are allotted to the earth's temporal existence (D & C 77:6; Revelation, chapters 6 and 7); Satan will be bound for one thousand years (D & C 88:110, Revelation 20:2), and the earth will rest one thousand years (Moses 7:64); the righteous are promised to live and reign with Christ for one thousand years (Revelation 20:4). If Christ opened the fifth seal by being born at A.D. 1, and if the present calendar is correct (D & C 20:1 is a pretty good indication that it may be), then Christ has to come in the year 2,000. Another piece of information used in this reasoning is that father Lehi knew the exact year of the coming of the Lord on earth, and dated his exodus from Jerusalem at exactly six hundred years B.C. This is a pretty good argument, and there is evidence that this may be correct. This must, however, be considered as only a theory with limited circumstantial evidence. Many scholars have determined that the exactness of the present calendar should be considered in only approximate terms.

Even if the present dating of time is correct, one must also look at some other considerations:
1. When did Christ open his seal? Was it when he was born, A.D. 1? When he was of an accountable age, eight? When he first taught in the temple at age twelve? When he began his ministry at age thirty? When he finished his earthly work and was resurrected? Or even when he returned to teach as the first fruits of the resurrection?
2. In the closing of the sixth seal and the opening of the seventh, some of the events seem to overlap, appearing in both seals, like the breaking of a new day, when the difference between night and day is imprecise. This overlap leaves room at the end of the one thousand years of the millennium for Satan's little season, a period of time where Satan is loosed to yet attempt one last challenge of Christ's authority.
3. As stated in Revelation 8:2, and 11:15, it is apparent that Christ comes after the opening of the seventh seal. However, John does not tell just how long after. The Savior taught the ancient disciples that the day and hour of Christ's coming was information known only to the Father (Matthew 24:36). Paul teaches, however, that the children of light will be watching and prepared when he comes (1 Thessalonians 5:1-6).
4. The last and most important clue is given in Revelation 19:7, which tells that the marriage of the Lamb will take place when his bride has made herself ready. The early Latter-day Saints were promised that the time would be cut short in righteousness (D & C 84:97; 109:59). It may just be that today's saints hold the key. Christ will come when his people are ready to receive him. Moroni taught that one can receive no witness until after the trial of his faith. Christ came to people in the ancient Americas only after they had faith in him (Ether 12:6, 7). Christ is expected to come spectacularly in the clouds of heaven, and as the morning sun that shines from east to west and fills the whole earth (Joseph Smith Matthew 1:26). Such an event is described in Revelation 11:15 and Zechariah 14:3-4, as Christ sets foot on the Mount of Olives and shows himself to the Jewish nation.

If Third Nephi is a type for the second coming, one can also watch for many comings to groups and individuals. From D & C 133:19-21, it is shown that Christ shall stand upon the mount of Olivet, the mighty ocean, the islands of the sea, and upon the land of Zion. His voice shall be heard among all people. Chapter 7 of this book shows that the 144,000 have their calling and election made sure. This includes the promised Second Comforter, which is Jesus Christ, personally. This then constitutes a coming of Christ to those individuals. Also described are the comings of Christ to Adam-Ondi-Ahman, as well as his coming to some church leaders, and coming suddenly to his temple (Malachi 3:1).

The Book of Mormon, compiled by prophets who had seen this day, helps reveal the times and seasons in relation to the second coming of Christ. Like a kindly, righteous and prophetic grandparent who lovingly relates his life experiences to guide and answer the dilemmas of a troubled youth, the Book of Mormon should be read more as a guidebook than just a history. During the April 1987 General Conference, President Ezra Taft Benson gave a powerful talk titled "The Savior's Visit to America." In this address he said:

> The record of the Nephite history just prior to the Savior's visit reveals many parallels to our day as we anticipate the Savior's second coming. What a blessing it would be if every family would read together Third Nephi, discuss its sacred contents, and then determine how they can liken it unto themselves and apply its teachings.

Immediately after that conference, the author began to read Third Nephi—not as a distant and dusty history, but as if seeing the unfolding of events in this day. A powerful witness and insight came, tears were shed for the sins of that nation and also those today. All should rejoice with the righteous of Nephi's day and in the anticipated blessings of the present day. Most impressive was the speed with which important events transpired. In the latter days the time could be shortened even more.

It is known that in the last day, all flesh will see certain events of the second coming together (Revelation 1:7, Isaiah 40:5, D & C 101:23). These events will parallel the darkness, voices, thunders and earthquakes universally experienced in the Americas at AD 34. The most important event in the Book of Mormon was Christ's coming to the Nephites following the destruction. It will be remembered that the first visitation to the Nephites and personal teaching of the Savior came sometime after the destructions, as a group gathered at the temple in the land of Bountiful to marvel, wonder, and show each other the great and marvelous change that had taken place (3 Nephi 11:1). This was not seen by all the people of the Americas at once. Christ called twelve disciples and sent them forth. He told them that he had other sheep yet to visit, and came to others on several other recorded instances. Indian legend (*He Walked the Americas,*) tells that he went personally from village to village and traveled much among the people. His coming to the

Nephites at the temple in Bountiful is the only record of any of these many "comings" that could be classified as a spectacular coming from the clouds of heaven, yet to many other people and villages and even lands, he came!

The point is that the Lord commands his people to watch, lest they be caught unawares. He says that he will come at an hour when many are not expecting him. Even if the world knew the exact time of his coming, any person could be called home at any hour to meet him. The only safety is to be prepared and stay prepared. The Lord also commands his people, however, to study, that they may know the times, seasons, and signs, to increase their faith and personal readines.

11
Jerusalem's Prophets, Destruction and Deliverance

The study of chapter 11 begins with a different perspective of the events of the last days—from Jerusalem. John first is given the assignment to measure the Temple of God (Revelation 11:1-2). This tells of a temple in the Middle East when Christ comes. This temple is built to Judaic specifications, with an outer court of the gentiles. John is told not to measure the outer court, because it represents the portion where the gentiles are allowed to go. John also states that the gentiles will symbolically tread the Holy City underfoot forty and two months (three and one-half years).

Two Prophets with Great Power

John then shows that Christ has called two witnesses who are given power to prophesy one thousand, two hundred and three score days. This is just shy of three and one-half years that the gentiles will be treading the outer court of the temple underfoot. The two witnesses are likened to two olive trees. Olive trees are the source of the precious oil used to nourish, bless, anoint, and fill lamps and are difficult trees to uproot and move. The two are also referred to as candlesticks. Revelation 1 described candlesticks, which signified beings of light and glory. Christ was in the midst of these. Since they are introduced immediately after the measuring of the temple, it is logical that their work and habitation are in relationship to the temple. They have been given great power, reminiscent of the power given to Nephi before the coming of Christ to the Americas (Helaman 10:5). They have power to destroy, to curse, and to shut the heavens; and they have power over the actual elements.

When they have finished their testimony, the beast that ascends out of the bottomless pit makes war against them, overcomes them and kills them. Their bodies shall lie in the streets of the great city. This city is designated as the spiritual equivalent of Sodom and of Egypt, and was also the city where Christ was crucified. In a most disgraceful manner, the inhabitants of the earth will not allow their bodies to be buried, and so they will lie in the streets for three and a half days while the people rejoice, make merry, and even give gifts to each other. The rejoicing over the death of God's servants, and the mockery of their bodies, are a testimony against the wicked state of many still living on the earth. It is also interesting to note that only in this day could they that dwell on earth be kept apprised of the situation in such a timely fashion. It appears that the media will be functioning right up until the end.

After the three and one-half days, the spirit of life comes back into them (Revelation 11:11). A great voice calls them up to heaven. They ascend in a cloud, and all their enemies behold them. This is followed by a great earthquake, which destroys ten percent of the city and seven thousand men. The remainder, afraid, give glory to the God of Heaven.

Who are the two witnesses? Isaiah 51:18-20 and 2 Nephi 8:18-20 both teach that they are not from Jerusalem, but "come unto thee." They lie at the "head of the streets as a wild bull in a net." Historically, each of the twelve tribes has a banner that represents their tribe. The symbol of the tribe of Joseph is a bull. In D & C 77:15, the Lord reveals that they are not only witnesses, but also prophets:

> Q. What is to be understood by the two witnesses in the 11th chapter of Revelation?
> A. They are two prophets that are to be raised up to the Jewish nation in the last days at the time of the restoration, and to prophesy to the Jews after they are gathered and have built the city of Jerusalem in the land of their fathers.
>
> (D & C 77:15)

If the two witnesses are from the tribe of Joseph or, more specifically from the tribe of Ephraim, the mission and influence of these two prophets may be what finally breaks down the long standing barriers between Judah and Ephraim, as foretold in Isaiah 11:13: "The envy also of Ephraim shall depart, and the adversaries of Judah shall be cut off: Ephraim shall not envy Judah, and Judah shall not vex Ephraim."

Four Woes May Bypass Jerusalem

Note that chapter 11, which views the events from an Israeli perspective, begins with an unnumbered woe (the beast from the bottomless pit will make war against them). Then suddenly it states, "the second woe is past;

and . . . the third cometh quickly" (Revelation 11:14). This is followed by the sounding at the time of the seventh angel. Only two woes are mentioned leading up to the time of the sounding of the seventh angel. In other words, four woes or plagues may bypass the Land of Palestine. If Palestine appears more stable than the rest of the world, the effect might be the hastening to completion the gathering of the Jews out of the world to their land of inheritance and destiny.

Verse 18 is a description of "the great and dreadful day of the Lord," It is a day when all nations will be full of anger, and a day of judgment, for those who fear and love the Lord will be rewarded, and those who are destroying the earth will themselves be destroyed.

A Temple in Jerusalem

John concludes the chapter by drawing attention to the temple in heaven, which is now opened. So that there is no mistake about which temple, it is noted that this is the temple that contains the ark of his testament. The ark was originally carried in the portable temple or tabernacle. This cross-references very nicely with what Enoch prophesied in his last-days testament:

> And righteousness will I send down out of heaven; and truth will I send forth out of the earth, to bear testimony of mine Only Begotten; his resurrection from the dead; yea, and also the resurrection of all men; and righteousness and truth will I cause to sweep the earth as with a flood, to gather out mine elect from the four quarters of the earth, unto a place which I shall prepare, an Holy City, that my people may gird up their loins, and be looking forth for the time of my coming; for there shall be my *tabernacle,* and it shall be called Zion, a New Jerusalem.
>
> And the Lord said unto Enoch: Then shalt thou and all thy city meet them there, and we will receive them into our bosom, and they shall see us; and we will fall upon their necks, and they shall fall upon our necks, and we will kiss each other.
>
> (Moses 7:62-63)

The tabernacle is used as a type for Enoch's Zion, which is also portable. At the time of Noah there were two arks, one which carried Noah, his family, and creatures of the earth through to safety. The other ark was also a place of refuge for the righteous, even the city of Enoch. It is called the ark of the covenant because of God's covenant to Noah (Joseph Smith Translation, Genesis 9:21-25). The entire city is also a temple, because Christ dwells there among the people (Moses 7:69).

The author believes that the ark of the covenant carried by the hosts of Israel under Moses was an earthly reminder of the blessing of this previous covenant. From this special temple comes an endowment of knowledge and priesthood power. These keys of priesthood power are mentioned in the Joseph Smith Translation:

> For God having sworn unto Enoch and unto his seed with an oath by himself; that every one being ordained after this order and calling should have power, by faith, to break mountains, to divide the seas, to dry up waters, to turn them out of their course;
>
> To put at defiance the armies of nations, to divide the earth, to break every band, to stand in the presence of God; to do all things according to his will, according to his command, subdue principalities and powers; and this by the will of the Son of God which was from before the foundation of the world.
>
> (Joseph Smith Translation, Genesis 14:30, 31)

Two Cities Caught Up to Heaven

The scriptural references to "the temple in heaven, the tabernacle in heaven, ark of the covenant in heaven, rock of heaven, cloud, bow in the cloud, exceedingly high mountain, Mount Zion, and being caught up" may all be references to Enoch's city and/or the city of Salem, and the endowment of power received therefrom. This covenant is extremely important to the righteous living in the latter days because salvation from the final plague of the wicked coincides with a person's being reunited with Zion, the new Jerusalem. This reuniting can only occur on conditions of righteousness.

About the two ancient Zions, Enoch's and Melchizedek's, Orson Pratt had this to say:

> As the earth passes through its great last change, two of its principal cities—the Old Jerusalem of the eastern continent, and the new Jerusalem of the Western continent—will be preserved from the general conflagration, being caught up into heaven. These two cities, with all their glorified throng, will descend upon the redeemed earth, being the grand capitals of the new creation.
>
> (Orson Pratt, Journal of Discourses, Vol. 1, p. 332)

Melchizedek as a Type of the Second Coming

The distinction between the two returning heavenly Jerusalems was also plainly taught by the prophet Ether (Ether 13:3, 9-11).

The Topical Guide to the LDS Scriptures, under Melchizedek, cross-references to "Jesus Christ, Types of, in Anticipation." In other words, Melchizedek can be looked at as a forerunner and type of Christ, with many similarities. Who was Melchizedek? In the *Times and Seasons,* Volume 5, page 746, dated December 15, 1844, Elder John Taylor taught that Shem, the son of Noah, was Melchizedek. This gives a clue to look further at Melchizedek as perhaps more than a name—perhaps a title. In Hebrew, *melch* equals *king,* and *zoidok* equals *priest.* If pronounced phonetically together, it creates the word *Melchizedek*—the king and priest.

Note: Although there has been disagreement among LDS scholars as to this being his identity, the author is comfortable with this understanding (a fact that is incidental to the value obtained from this scripture). In D & C 138:41, Shem is referred to as the "great high priest." Melchizedek also carries that title (D & C 101:22). Shem, in Hebrew, can be translated as "The Name." Here are two contemporary references to an individual whose name seems to be a reference to something else.

Whenever a new dispensation is brought forth, the members of the Church are given the opportunity to accept the light of righteous government and divine priesthood leadership. The Lord longs to bless his people with both, for this is the kingdom of God on earth as it is in heaven. In contrast, when Satan controls both the spiritual and political kingdoms, this condition is spoken of as the "great and abominable Church"—Satan's kingdom and church together (1 Nephi 14:9-11). Notice from this scripture that the object of the great and abominable church is dominion over all the earth. This *dominion* would be possible only with the control of government. The author recommends H. Verlan Andersen's (formerly of the First Quorum of Seventy) excellent book, *The Great and Abominable Church of the Devil,* published by his sons and grandsons, Orem, UT, (801) 224-3368, for a more in-depth treatment of the subject of Satan's Church, including usurped authority and prostituted government. By contrast, under Jesus Christ, the political and spiritual will eventually be together, as he is both king as well as high priest, after the order of Melchizedek (Hebrews 6:20).

What did Melchizedek do? He gave blessings, he was a man of faith, he wrought righteousness, he had power over lions and stopped their mouths, he quenched the violence of fire. He was approved of God. He was ordained a high priest, after the order of Enoch, who was after the order of the Son of God. He called a people to come out of their wicked condition to seek Zion. He protected them by priesthood power and, like Enoch, eventually separated his city from the wicked world, as it was caught up to heaven and reserved unto the latter days (see Joseph Smith Translation, Genesis 14:25-40).

Melchizedek also blessed Abraham, collected tithes, and as a priest, brought forth the bread and wine. Melchizedek met Abraham after he returned from the slaughter of the kings, where he had liberated Sodom and Gomorrah and freed his nephew, Lot (Genesis 14). It is important to not overlook Sodom and Gomorrah, for this day, in many ways, is a likeness of theirs. They were once liberated by the Lord's servant. Angels came down to the city to seek out the righteous. When there were no righteous left, the wicked cities were burned with fire from heaven. This pattern of a spiritual, then physical, separation of the righteous from the wicked, through their faith and by the priesthood before calamity befalls, is well established through scripture.

12
Satan's Earthly Kingdoms

The entirety of chapter 12 is found in the Joseph Smith Translation accompanying the Bible printed by The Church of Jesus Christ of Latter-day Saints (p. 813). Studying this chapter from the Joseph Smith Translation will uncover many hidden truths; the church is blessed to have the original teachings of John restored through the Prophet Joseph. Once again, a shift in perspective is noted because John backs up to give an understanding of the identity of the enemy, the great red dragon, the Devil or Satan. To understand what is happening here, one must read this as it should have appeared.

It is little wonder that portions of this text are missing, or the order mixed, in the King James Version, since they contain a direct exposé of Satan. Only in John's cryptic writing can be found so much direct writing about Lucifer and his earthly kingdom in the Bible, and even here there is evidence of tampering.

Verse 7 teaches that there was an actual war in heaven between the forces of good, led by Michael and his angels, and the dragon and his angels of evil. The war ended with Satan and his followers being cast out of the celestial world, and eventually ending up in this telestial earth. Verse 4 shows that Satan was able to draw a full third of the heavenly host to follow him to this earth to make and continue the war with the seed of the woman.

A great sign is seen in heaven, a heavenly symbol that represents what actually occurs on earth. A woman, big with child and in pain, is about to deliver. Verse 7 shows that the woman is the church. It must be noted from verse 7 that this is an expanded definition of church, meaning those people, or groups of people, who are struggling, suffering, and laboring to bring forth the Kingdom of God on earth. This kingdom entails both the spiritual, as well as the political. Remember that the righteous are seeking a kingdom with Christ as king. The government will be upon his shoulders, and he will be their high priest.

Verses 2 and 3 show that out from among these early saints came a man child. The right to rule all nations belongs to him, and he will rule with a rod of iron. Nephi's dream demonstrates that the iron rod and the Word of God are interchangeable, so this provides an added perspective of these verses. This child was caught up unto God and his throne.

Verse 9 points out that the old serpent, called the Devil and Satan, is deceiving the whole world. To know what Satan is up to, one cannot rely on what is taught by the world, for the whole world lives in Satan's deception. Things of great import and of vast consequences are occurring in secret and are covered over by a veil of deception. The best hope is to be well-founded in the truth, which God has given in the form of the scriptures, to know and follow the prophets, to be spiritually schooled by the Holy Ghost, and to search for truth and reject all the error which the deceiver pours out.

With the casting out of Satan from heaven came salvation, strength, the kingdom of God and the power of Christ into that sphere. Only when Satan was gone could this harmony, peace, and the salvation of God abide, even in that exalted existence. It appears that one of the reasons that heaven is heaven is not only who is there, but also who is not there.

The Personality of Satan

In verse 10 the devil is called the accuser. He is not a builder, but a destroyer. His accusations were continual, day and night. Satan has managed, somehow, in his own mind, to justify this constant stream of accusations. For thousands of years, Satan has carried a grudge against mankind's perfect Lord and Savior, Jesus Christ.

John teaches that the job is not yet done. Though the heavens rejoice, a woe is pronounced upon this earth, because the devil is come down unto earth, full of great wrath. Satan is working with a knowledge that even here, he has but a short time. Michael, as the man Adam, and his earthly followers will yet finish the job of once again casting Satan out.

A profound scripture is found in verse 11. It teaches what it takes to overcome Satan. He is overcome by three great keys: first, the blood of the Lamb; second, the word of testimony; and third, a love that exceeds even the love of one's own life.

The Church Flees to the Wilderness

Chapter 12 contains another allegorical image. After the dragon persecutes the woman (or church) following the birth of the man-child (Christ), the woman was given two wings of a great eagle, to flee into the wilderness. The author believes the image of fleeing oppression and the image of the wilderness all fit with the migration of righteous people to America. The eagle is an easily recognized symbol of America's freedom. Also, the continents of North and South America, when viewed from above, bear a striking resemblance to wings.

In this "wilderness" the church is nourished for a time, and times, and half a time from the face of the serpent. If it is assumed that a time is something people of this day would relate to, then one-hundred year periods would work well with John's prophecy and with American history. A time (possibly one hundred years?), plus times (meaning plural, probably two hundred years), plus half a time (fifty years), equals three hundred fifty years. This is a very good approximation for the time that America has been a place of refuge for those seeking to bring forth the kingdom of God. The Pilgrims, seeking to establish a kingdom of God, arrived in 1620.

A Lesson from the Colonization of America

An interesting lesson comes from Americas history about the pilgrims. All of the founding fathers were very familiar with this lesson, but it is seldom mentioned today. Understanding this lesson about the earliest beginnings of American colonization helps to see how God brought about a national condition where the church could the nourished for the three hundred fifty years the author believes John is referring to. This also points out the differences between God's kingdom and the kingdom of Satan, and bears repeating.

As these early god-fearing people were contemplating their desire to begin to establish a kingdom of God on earth, and in their love for one another, they sat in the *Mayflower* off the coast of New England. They had time for philosophy. The London Company, sponsors of the colony, had mandated a socialistic order. Many of the pilgrims had stayed in England, refusing to sign such a mandate. Since they had missed the Virginia drop-off point, and had mistakenly landed in the harsh climate of New England, many pilgrims who did go felt that they were no longer bound by this part of their agreement.

They did, however, in the spirit of good faith, agree to give the experiment a try. Everyone was to work for the good of everyone else. Either all would succeed or no one would. These were noble and seemingly generous ideals. God teaches that one should be able to judge by the fruits. What were the fruits of this philosophical experiment? Three hard years of near starvation. The anticipated blessings from heaven seemed to withhold themselves. Unless something was done, the colony would have to shut down or die off.

By vote and common consent, the rights of property and laws of prosperity were restored. The individual was, first, to be responsible to govern and take care of himself—of course, without disturbing his neighbor. He was next to take responsibility for his family, followed by a responsibility for the colony. Strong people make strong families, which make strong communities. It just doesn't work when tried backwards. As if by flood, the blessings of heaven began to pour forth. From this moment on, the colony was a thriving success.

If John's record teaches that the woman or church shall be nourished in the wilderness for three hundred and fifty years, then the nourishment began when the principles of righteous government were in place, not when they arrived with their socialistic, albeit good, intentions. This period of time would end in about 1973. Now the church would have to stand on its own strength. This socialistic nation would be a drain, rather than a source of nourishment, from that point on. Nourishment never comes from the government (unless the government has legally plundered it from someone else); but the principles of freedom have allowed the church to be nourished in the land. This nation's forefathers were well aware of this great lesson, and referred to it often in their establishment of the founding principles of this nation.

This is also one of the great lessons from the temple. If a person can govern himself, he will be worthy to be endowed with blessings from God. This should lead to additional stewardship. He is then worthy to be blessed, with the sanction and blessings of God, to be a governor over his family. If he is able to be a successful governor over himself and his family, using the principles of righteousness, he will be worthy and will be blessed to be a governor in the kingdom of God.

Only the Righteous Should Govern

Early church leaders were chastised by the Lord for their emphasis on church work at the neglect of governing and leading in their own homes.

Most people know of the problems when men, unable to govern themselves, find themselves in position of authority over others. I Timothy 3:1-7 teaches the qualifications for a bishop:

> This is a true saying, If a man desire the office of a bishop, he desireth a good work.
>
> A bishop then must be blameless, the husband of one wife, vigilant, sober, of good behavior, given to hospitality, apt to teach;
>
> Not given to wine, no striker, not greedy of filthy lucre; but patient, not a brawler, not covetous;
>
> One that ruleth well his own house, having his children in subjection with all gravity;
>
> (For if a man know not how to rule his own house, how shall he take care of the church of God?)
>
> Not a novice, lest being lifted up with pride he fall into the condemnation of the devil.
>
> Moreover he must have a good report of them which are without; lest he fall into reproach and the snare of the devil.

Since the kingdom of God on earth, as it is in heaven, includes the political, as well as the spiritual, these are also qualifications necessary for those who would be governmental leaders. A man who cannot govern himself or his family in righteousness should not be trusted to be a governor over a nation, state, or anyone else.

Look to a System's Fruits

In speaking to a group of socialists in France, Apostle John Taylor taught that they should look to the fruits to determine the value of a system (*Journal of Discourses,* Vol. 5, pp. 237-238). The saints, in a few short years, had taken a worthless piece of swamp ground on a wide bend of the Mississippi River, and converted it into the largest and most beautiful city in the state of Illinois. This city was built under conditions of immense poverty and persecution. When asked how it was done, the Prophet Joseph Smith replied, "I teach them correct principles and they govern themselves."

In contrast, this same group of socialists Apostle Taylor was addressing had sent a well-funded colony to Nauvoo. He said to them:

"You have sent out to Nauvoo a number of your most intellectual men, well provided with means of every kind and with talent of the first order. Now what is the result? They have gone to a place that we have deserted; they found houses built, gardens and farms enclosed, nothing to do but to take possession of them?"

"Yes. They found buildings of all kinds, public and private, in which they could live and congregate."

"Yes. Was there ever a people better situated in regard to testing your natural philosophy? You could not have hit upon a better place. It is a fertile country, on the banks of the most magnificent stream in the United States—the Mississippi. Houses built, gardens made, fields enclosed and cultivated. You have wise men among you—the wisest, the creme de la creme of your society, yet with all this and the favorable circumstances under which your people commenced there, what have you done? Every time that I take up a paper of yours the cry from there is, 'Send us means'; 'we want means'; 'we are in difficulty'; 'we want more money.' 'This is their eternal cry, is it not?"

"Yes."

"Now," said I, "on the other hand, we left our farms, houses, gardens, fields, orchards, and everything we had, except what we took along in the shape of food, seeds, farming utensils, wagons, carts, and we wandered for from ten to fifteen hundred miles, with hand-carts, ox teams and any way we could, and settled, finally, among the red savages of the forest. We had no fields to go to and no houses built; when we went there it was a desert—a howling wilderness, and the natives with which we were surrounded were as savage as the country itself. Now then, what is the result? We have only been there a few years, but what are we doing? We are sending money to bring in our emigration; we are sending hundreds of thousands of dollars, and have expended half a million a year in teams to bring in our poor from the nations. But what of you wise men who know not God, and think you know better than He does, what are you doing—you philosophers, intelligent men and philanthropists, crying out eternally, 'Send us help?' Which is the best?"

Said he, "Mr. Taylor, I have nothing to say."

(*Journal of Discourses,* Vol. 13, pp. 228-229.)

This continual plea for more money is echoed by today's socialists. After a few short years, the colony was disbanded in utter failure.

Karl Marx is a case in point. Unable to support or take care of himself without the charity of others, he married. In squalor, filth, confusion, and poverty, he became a father. In 1862, Marx wrote: "Daily my wife tells me she wishes she were lying in the grave with the children, and truly, I cannot blame her." Yet this small, evil, wicked man aspired to be a great one; and this, no less, by revolutionary force.

The socialist Adolf Hitler (likewise a small, evil, wicked man) was exalted as national leader. He held his power by placing in authority under him equally small and despotic individuals. This is the curse of the wicked. Isaiah 3:45 reads:

> And I will give children to be their princes, and babes shall rule over them.
>
> And the people shall be oppressed, every one by another, and every one by his neighbour: the child shall behave himself proudly against the ancient, and the base against the honourable.

This artificial elevation of base individuals is the great appeal of Satan's plan. This is truly why hell is hell. Satan's whole scheme is to accomplish by force what the Lord does by love and freely given service. A heaven, or Zion, is never built by force.

Only when a person has control of his property can he fulfill the commandment to be a wise steward. Without ownership, it is impossible to be generous, or to give, or to share, or to sacrifice, or even to be free and independent with rights of choice. It has been observed that even very small children can be remarkably generous and giving if they know that they have property rights over their own things. If they wish to share, it is their choice. Of course, teaching, praise, and encouragement are also very helpful. Along with this respect for what the child owns and is steward over must come a respect for what belongs to others. Many have seen parents grab a favorite toy from the arms of a crying child, demanding that he has to share. Force and coercion are used to teach the child that he can hold it, but it really isn't his. This always seems to foster the "mine, mine, mine" cry. By contrast, observe a child, just as adamant about the control of his toys, being told that "Yes, the toys are yours, and you do not have to share, but it would make your parents very pleased if you would. If you do share, you will probably find others just as willing to share with you." It usually only takes a few moments for even the smallest child to discover the joys of giving. The whole spirit of the exchange is completely different. Oh, that governments could learn this simple, basic lesson of life.

13
The Image and Mark of the Beast

In the premortal world, all knew Satan as a brother. A morning star, he must have been charismatic and persuasive to talk one-third of the hosts of heaven out of their agency. Satan became a vengeful, jealous power-monger; he defiantly flung to the Father his goal to rule all. Because the veil was drawn at birth, firsthand knowledge of Satan was forgotten, but his character is revealed through scripture and modern revelation, and his character has not changed. He still desires to rob the children of God of their agency. It is necessary to keep this knowledge in mind in order to see clearly his work and kingdom in today's world. Verse 1 is a critical scripture in understanding the remainder of the chapter. The most important line is missing from the text, but has been restored through the Joseph Smith Translation: *"And I saw another sign in the likeness of the kingdoms of the earth: a beast rise up out of the sea."*

Understanding Symbols of the Beast

The beast John described represents, and is, a symbol, or sign, of earthly kingdoms. The content of this chapter plainly shows that they are controlled by Satan. It is important to study these descriptions carefully to be able to recognize the adversary's work and avoid the deceiving of the whole earth that Satan has accomplished. Observe that most of the writings in John's Revelation center around the events of the last day; this chapter is no exception. Given specifically for the rightious living in the last days, the concepts herein will help accomplish their mission. This is often the first place many readers turn to in the Book of Revelation, but the complexity can be discouraging. Compare these symbols to looking at a schematic diagram. Only in looking at the individual components and their interrelation does one see the total picture.

In drama, the costumes, posture, and manner of speaking all clue the audience to the type of personality the actor is portraying. So it is with the characters introduced by John. His descriptions are clues, and these apocryphal characters will reveal who they really are through careful analysis. What John describes is of the utmost importance.

In verse 1, John begins to describe a beast. The beast has seven heads and ten horns. Perhaps all understanding of the significance of the heads and horns is difficult (more on this can be found in Revelation 17:9-14, and chapter 17 of this book), but make this observation: this is the same configuration as on the dragon that fought against Michael in the premortal war (Revelation 12:13). If chapter 13 deals with Satan's earthly kingdoms, as the author believes, it is logical to assume that Satan would set up his earthly kingdom in the image of his pre-earth kingdom. Somehow, the beast has picked up three more crowns than he wore in the pre-earth war. Upon the beast's heads is written the name of blasphemy. Dictionaries define the word *blasphemy* as the crime of assuming to oneself the rights and qualities of God. This Satanic kingdom of the devil poses as that which is good and righteous. True to character, Satan attempts to replace God.

The Earthly Identity of the Beast

The author believes that the identity of the beast spoken of by John is Communism, and will proceed to submit many evidences to support his conclusion. The remainder of this book operates under this premise. The author invites readers to carefully consider John's prophecies and the evidences offered in this and other books when forming their own beliefs.

In verse 2 the beast is likened to a leopard. Leopards are considered the stealthiest of all animals. Very seldom are their comings and goings seen, except by the most expert of observers. Usually leopards are seen more from the unmistakable work they leave behind rather than sightings of the actual beast. Without their trail of destruction, it would be easy to deny their actual existence.

The beast also has the feet of a bear. Look for an earthly kingdom that leaves bear tracks; the great Russian Bear comes immediately to mind. The beast has a mouth as the mouth of a lion. The lion is as a symbol for the tribe of Judah. Karl Marx, who was of Jewish ancestry, has been known as the mouthpiece of communism. The lion has always been used as the symbol of power, and also destruction. Since it is the mouth that is featured, expect to see that the beast has a voracious appetite. According to *Guiness Book of World Records,* (1994 version, pp. 174-175) over 100 million people have been murdered by the communists this century. Another description of the same beast is found in Revelation 17:3, where another identifying feature is described: the beast is scarlet in color. One can easily see who the beast is when asked who the reds are!

If the Red Communists are this beast warned of by John, the words of modern prophets should also sound a similar warning. A statement from President David O. McKay, given at the priesthood session of the April 1966 General Conference, reads: "The position of this Church on the subject of communism has never changed. We consider it the greatest satanical threat to peace, prosperity, and the spread of God's work among man that exists on the face of the earth." This statement is repeated in full in the appendix of President Benson's powerful book *An Enemy Hath Done This*. The *greatest threat* to God's work is what this beast is all about.

So that no mistake is made, it is once again stated that the dragon is the giver of his power, dwelling place, and great authority. Since free agency is God's greatest gift, it makes sense that in Satan's opposing kingdom, his main goal would be to marshall forces to take that freedom away.

Wounding and Healing of the Beast

Verse 3 describes a very startling world event. One of the beast's heads is wounded unto death. A surprising parallel can be found in recent history, as the world has witnessed what the media has touted as the "death of communism." But wait—before John even finishes his sentence, he states that his deadly wound was healed. This apparent resurrection from the dead causes all the world to wonder after the beast. How could this be possible? Only one head of this multiheaded beast was wounded unto death. Later, John describes a relationship between the beast and the latter-day whore, Babylon. This relationship could be tied to the miraculous healing of the beast.

Verse 7 shows that the beast will make war with the saints. There will be a short period of time when his power will extend over all kindreds and tongues and nations; with the exception of those whose names are written in the Lamb's book of life, the entire earth will look to communism/socialism for their salvation. The author believes this is what is meant by "they shall worship him." John feels it is critical that to pay attention; he pauses and uses those familiar words and invitation of Christ: "If any man have an ear, let him hear" (Revelation 13:9).

It is sobering to learn that even now, there is justice. Those who would conspire to take the liberty of others, the behind-the-scenes supporters of this great iniquity, must themselves go into captivity. The wicked that would kill with the sword must be killed with the sword. This period of earthly turmoil will try both the patience and the faith of the saints.

A Second Beast Speaks to the World

Following this understanding of the first beast, John shows that it does not act alone. A second, collaborating beast is also on the scene. This beast comes out of the earth. He has two horns like a lamb's, and he speaks as a dragon. There are three important components here: first, the earth, or world; second, a lamb, often used as a symbol of peace; and third, speech like a dragon, or Satan. John does not say that the beast is a lamb, although that is the deceptive image put forth. Rather, he focuses on the lamb's horns. He could be saying that the beast is armed. The two horns could have similar meaning to the ten horns of the beast described in Revelation 17:12; if so, the horns would be two kings, kingdoms, or divisions of power, such as an East-West division of power.

What would one expect the speech of a dragon to be like? The author believes it would be deceptive, lying, power-seeking, secret and in the dark, with a major thrust to usurp the free agency of its followers with the promise of salvation, deliverance, and protection. Since the speech of the second beast is one of its prominent characteristics, and the only one that describes what it actually does and not only what it looks like, look for a world organization noted for its speech that promotes the works of the dragon. Revelation 13:5 shows that one of the keys of power given to the first beast (the Red Communists) is the fact that it was given a mouth to speak great things. Consider what world organization has given the Communists a podium from which to speak to the world.

This second beast also gets his power from the dragon. His mission is to cause those that dwell upon the earth to worship the first beast, whose deadly wound was healed. The word *worship* is a very powerful word, but assume that John chose his wording carefully. When one worships the Lord in a church, he is expected to:

1. Support the kingdom financially
2. Learn the principles
3. Accept and follow the examples of leaders
4. Embrace and support the work

Does any other last days entity so perfectly fit the criteria given by John for this second beast as the United Nations? President Ezra Taft Benson had this to say in a chapter titled "The United Nations—Planned Tyranny," found in *An Enemy Hath Done This,* which the author recommends to all truth seekers:

It has always been a source of amazement to me how so many Americans properly are concerned over the growth of big government and the welfare state here at home, but continue to give their unqualified support to the U.N. which incorporates every doctrine which they abhor. The reason, I suppose, is that too few of us have taken the time or felt the need to find out just what is the concept of government at the U.N.

President Benson has cautioned that the world must "separate the dream of nations united from the reality of the United Nations and objectively look at our existing U.N.," for by their fruits shall ye know them (*An Enemy Hath Done This,* p. 202). What are some of the fruits of the United Nations? Never forget that the Korean and Vietnam wars were tragedies entered into, not by congressionally declared acts of war as the U.S. Constitution authorizes, but under the umbrella of the U.N. The wholesale slaughter in Katanga, a little African nation struggling for freedom several years ago was documented by impartial humanitarian observers, such as the Red Cross, to have been augmented and even perpetrated by the U.N. "peace-keeping" forces. More recently, the Muslims in Bosnia have been subjected to outright genocide and have strongly criticized the U.N. for its presence and actions in their country. They have repeatedly tried to alert the rest of the world that the U.N. forces have done nothing to stop the slaughter; they have only prevented the Muslims from getting hold of the arms and ammunition they need and would gladly use to defend themselves.

Earl Browder, general secretary of the Communist Party, USA, stated in his book *Victory and After,* (New York International Publishers, 1942), "The American Communists worked energetically and tirelessly to lay the foundations for the United Nations." He further stated, "It can be said, without exaggeration, that ever closer relations between our nation and the Soviet Union are an unconditional requirement for the United Nations as a world coalition" (*Victory and After,* p. 160).

The Communist/Soviet spy and top State Department infiltrator Alger Hiss was the United Nation's first Secretary General (a post he filled by appointment prior to the actual acceptance of the U.N. Charter, as reported in *Time Magazine,* April 16, 1945), and was one of the authors of its charter. (Remember that this is the same time period when the United State's atomic bomb secrets were being stolen.) The top military post in the U.N., in charge of all U.N. military activities, has always been filled by a Communist. All but one have come from the USSR. The United Nations has been recognized

THE IMAGE AND MARK OF THE BEAST

as a great Trojan horse by both Communists as well as informed Americans; J. Edgar Hoover tirelessly warned our country that the U.N. is not only an "occasional haven for a Soviet agent, but the center of communist espionage in America!" (*An Enemy Hath Done This*, p. 205). Communist U.N. agents are given a safe base of operation, status above the law, diplomatic immunity, a bountiful salary (of which U.S. taxpayers foot 25 percent), free access to the U.S. patent office, industrial centers, and leaders. Through the United Nations the world has accepted the communist vote and veto, and they have used this veto privilege over a hundred times, while the U.S. is yet to use it once.

The United Nations has given the Communists a legitimate platform to voice their propaganda. J. Reuben Clark, while serving as a U.S. Ambassador, carefully studied the U.N. Charter and had this to say:

> . . . there is no provision in the Charter itself that contemplates ending war. It is true the Charter provides for force to bring peace, but such use of force is itself war . . . .
>
> The Charter is built to prepare for war, not to promote peace . . . .
> The Charter is a war document not a peace document . . . .

Ambassador Clark further predicted:

> Not only does the Charter Organization not prevent future wars, but it makes it practically certain that we shall have future wars, and as to such wars it takes from us the power to declare them, to choose the side on which we shall fight, to determine what forces and military equipment we shall use in the war, and to control and command our sons who do the fighting."
>
> (*The United Nations Conspiracy*, p. 35.)

The oft-repeated sentiment that the U.N. is the world's last and best hope for peace is in itself proof of the Book of Revelation prophecy that the second beast would cause "them which dwell on earth to worship after the first beast" (Revelation 13:12). Christ, the only true hope for peace, is replaced by an earthly counterfeit institution that promises world peace, which only the Savior can bring.

John gives one last parting image: "He doeth great wonders, so that he maketh fire come down from heaven on the earth in the sight of men" (Revelation 13:13). The whole world recently watched in awe as U.N. "peace-keeping" forces in the Persian Gulf used seemingly miraculous weapons to bring down fire from heaven.

The Beasts Flourish Today

Neither the first nor second beasts, which represent earthly satanic kingdoms in this day, are dead, but rather, as President Benson testified in October Conference, 1988, "more highly organized, more cleverly disguised, and more powerfully promoted than ever before. Secret combinations lusting for power, gain, and glory are flourishing. A secret combination that seeks to overthrow the freedom of all lands, nations, and countries is increasing its evil influence and control over America and the entire world." He then referred church members to Ether 8:18-25:

> And it came to pass that they formed a secret combination, even as they of old; which combination is most abominable and wicked above all, in the sight of God;
> For the Lord worketh not in secret combinations, neither doth he will that man should shed blood, but in all things hath forbidden it, from the beginning of man.
> And now I, Moroni, do not write the manner of their oaths and combinations, for it hath been made known unto me that they are had among all people, and they are had among the Lamanites.
> And they have caused the destruction of this people of whom I am now speaking, and also the destruction of the people of Nephi.
> And whatsoever nation shall uphold such secret combinations, to get power and gain, until they shall spread over the nation, behold, they shall be destroyed; for the Lord will not suffer that the blood of his saints, which shall be shed by them, shall always cry unto him from the ground for vengeance upon them and yet he avenge them not.
> Wherefore, O ye Gentiles, it is wisdom in God that these things should be shown unto you, that thereby ye may repent of your sins, and suffer not that these murderous combinations shall get above you, which are built up to get power and gain—and the work, yea, even the work of destruction come upon you, yea, even the sword of the justice of the Eternal God shall fall upon you, to your overthrow and destruction if ye shall suffer these things to be.
> Wherefore, the Lord commandeth you, *when ye shall see these things come among you that ye shall awake to a sense of your awful situation,* because of this secret combination which shall be among you; or wo be unto it, because of the blood of them who have been slain; for they cry from the dust for vengeance upon it, and also upon those who built it up.

For it cometh to pass that *whoso buildeth it up seeketh to overthrow the freedom of all lands, nations, and countries; and it bringeth to pass the destruction of all people,* for it is built up by the devil, who is the father of all lies; even that same liar who beguiled our first parents, yea, even that same liar who hath caused man to commit murder from the beginning; who hath hardened the hearts of men that they have murdered the prophets, and stoned them, and cast them out from the beginning.

This nation will suffer for its sins, especially its pride, which causes many to raise up, support, and be blinded to the secret combinations in the present day. President Benson reiterated in his landmark conference address on pride Moroni's warning in Moroni 8:27, that it was the pride of the Nephites that proved their destruction. The Lords warning in the *Doctrine and Covenants* is to "Beware of pride, lest ye become as the Nephites of old" (D & C 38:39).

Every single latter-day prophet has denounced and clearly taught against the evils of communism/socialism. It is essential to make correct choices between God's agency and Satan's socialism. To help, the Lord has provided his word through his prophets:

Joseph Smith

Wednesday, 13.—I attended a lecture at the Grove, by Mr. John Finch, a Socialist, from England, and said a few words in reply . . . .

Thursday, 14. I attended a second lecture on Socialism, by Mr. Finch; and after he got through, I made a few remarks, alluding to Sidney Rigdon and Alexander Campbell getting up a community at Kirtland, and of the big fish there eating up all the little fish. I said I did not believe the doctrine. (*History of the Church,* Vol. 6, p. 33)

Brigham Young

We heard Brother Taylor's exposition of what is called Socialism this morning. What can they do? Live on each other and beg. It is a poor, unwise and very imbecile people who cannot take care of themselves. (*Journal of Discourses,* Vol. 14, p. 21)

John Taylor

I am sorry to see this murderous influence prevailing throughout the world, and perhaps this may be a fitting occasion to refer to some of these matters. The manifestations of turbulence and uneasiness which prevail among the nations of the earth are truly lamentable. Well, have

I anything to do with them? Nothing; but I cannot help but know that they exist. These feelings, which tend to do away with all right, rule, and government, and correct principles are not from God, or many of them are not. This feeling of communism and nihilism, aimed at the overthrow of rulers and men in position and authority, arises from a spirit of diabolism, which is contrary to every principle of the Gospel of the Son of God. But then do not the Scriptures say that these things shall occur? Yes. Do not the scriptures say that men shall grow worse and worse, deceiving and being deceived? Yes. Do not the scriptures tell us that thrones shall be cast down and empires destroyed and the rule and government of the earth be trodden under foot? Yes. But I cannot help but sympathize with those who suffer from their influences, while these afflictions are the result of wickedness and corruption, yet we cannot shut our eyes to the fact that those who engage in these pernicious practices are exceedingly low, brutal, wicked and degraded. I would say "my soul come not thou into their secret; unto their assembly, mine honor, be not thou united." (*Journal of Discourses,* Vol. 22, p. 142)

Wilford Woodruff

You may wish to know why I make these remarks. I will tell you. Because God himself grants this right to every human being upon the earth irrespective of race or color; it is part of the divine economy not to force any man to heaven, not to coerce the mind but to leave it free to act for itself. He lays before His creature man the everlasting Gospel, the principles of life and salvation, and then leaves him to choose for himself or to reject for himself, with the definite understanding that he becomes responsible to Him for the results of his acts. (*Journal of Discourses,* Vol 23, p. 77)

Lorenzo Snow

In things that pertain to celestial glory there can be no forced operations. We must do according as the Spirit of the Lord operates upon our understandings and feelings. We cannot be crowded into matters, however great might be the blessing attending such procedure. We cannot be forced into living a celestial law; we must do this ourselves, of our own free will. And whatever we do in regard to the principle of the United Order, we must do it because we desire to do it. (*Journal of Discourses,* Vol. 19, p. 346)

Joseph F. Smith

We must choose righteous men, good men to fill these positions. Hence, if you will only get good men to fill these offices, no one should care who they are, so that you have agreed upon them, and were one. We want you to be one both in temporal, political and religious things, in fact, in everything you put your hands to in righteousness. We want you to be one, one as God and Christ are one, seeing eye to eye. Do not try to crush anybody, or build yourselves up at the expense of your neighbor. Do not do it; it is a custom of the world, and it is a wrong principle. (*Journal of Discourses,* Vol. 25, p. 251)

Heber J. Grant

We condemn the outcome which wicked and designing men are now planning, namely: the worldwide establishment and perpetuation of some form of Communism on the one side, or of some form of Nazism or Fascism on the other. Each of these systems destroys liberty, wipes out free institutions, blots out free agency, stifles free press and free speech, crushes out freedom of religion and conscience. Free peoples cannot and do not survive under these systems. Free peoples the world over will view with horror the establishment of either Communism or Nazism as a worldwide system. Each system is fostered by those who deny the right and the ability of the common people to govern themselves. We proclaim that the common people have both this right and this ability. (*Messages of the First Presidency,* Vol. 6, p. 183)

George Albert Smith

Consider the condition in the world, the number who are determined to take from the rich man not what belongs to themselves, but that which belongs to the others. God has permitted men to get wealth, and if they obtained it properly, it is theirs, and he will bless them in its use if they will use it properly . . . .

We must not fall into the bad habits of other people. We must not get into the frame of mind that we will take what the other man has. Refer back to the ten commandments, and you will find one short paragraph, "Thou shalt not covet." That is what is the matter with a good many people today. They are coveting what somebody else has, when as a matter of fact, many of them have been cared for and provided with means to live by those very ones from whom they would take property. (*Prophets, Principles and National Survival,* p. 343,)

David O. McKay

We are placed on this earth to work, to live; and the earth will give us a living. It is our duty to strive to make a success of what we possess—to till the earth, subdue matter, conquer the globe, take care of the cattle, the flocks and the herds. It is the Government's duty to see that you are protected in these efforts, and no other man has the right to deprive you of any of your privileges. But it is not the Government's duty to support you. That is one reason why I shall raise my voice as long as God gives me sound or ability, against this Communistic idea that the Government will take care of us all, and everything belongs to the Government. It is wrong! No wonder, in trying to perpetuate that idea, they become anti-Christ, because that doctrine strikes directly against the doctrine of the Savior . . . .

No government owes you a living. You get it yourself by your own acts!—never by trespassing upon the rights of a neighbor; never by cheating him. You put a blemish upon your character the moment you do. (*Statements on Communism and the Constitution of the United States,* p. 23)

During the first half of the twentieth century we have traveled far into the soul-destroying land of socialism. (*Gospel Ideals,* p. 273)

Joseph Fielding Smith

We have all been taught the doctrine of personal free agency and that no individual is ever compelled by force or other means to comply with divine edicts and philosophy. We have been informed that a long time ago in the pre-existence there was a rebellion in heaven, and because one notable character, who had been entrusted with great authority, rebelled and led many away with him, he had to be cast out of the kingdom. However we should remember that every principle and law existing in the celestial kingdom has been proved to be perfect through the eternities through which they have come. If any individual proves himself worthy for the exaltation in that kingdom, it will be by strict obedience to every principle and covenant here existing. Therefore we may be assured that every law and principle thereunto pertaining is perfect and cannot be amended or discarded because of its perfection. (*Answers to Gospel Questions,* Vol. 4, p. 69)

The modern trend of the nation is towards dictatorship. It is taking form in two great camps, but, nevertheless, the direction is the same, although it is being reached by different routes. On the one side the direction to make an end of all nations, is through communism. (*The Progress of Man*, p. 397)

Harold B. Lee

There are some things of which I am sure, and that is that contrary to the belief and mistaken ideas of some people, the United Order will not be a socialistic or communistic setup; . . . (*Stand Ye in Holy Places*, p. 280)

Spencer W. Kimball

Granted all this, that there is much bitterness, hatred, class and race distinction, inequalities, and suffering in the world, are you wise in your determination to attack the problems as you seem to have in mind? Granted that men should all be free, should be equal, should be secure, should be fed and clothed, are you going about it in the right way? Is not any revolutionary movement which you might join or lead only a means to an end? Is it the proper means? If I read the scriptures with understanding, I see the Creator of this world denouncing all the evils which you hate and which you would overcome, but attempting to solve the problems in a different way. Did not the same evils of hate and greed and selfishness and avarice, and inequality and oppression and slavery exist to an even greater degree perhaps when the Maker of the world walked the earth? The enlightened and scripture-reading Jews expected him to come as a revolutionary, as a politician; as a warrior who would rid them of their oppressors, and bring them peace and plenty. Because he chose to handle the situation in a different way, they rejected him and nailed him to a great timber . . . .

He saw the bitterness of race hatreds and forthwith went into hated Samaria. He sat at the well and conversed with the despised Samaritan against common custom, for as the woman said, "The Jews have no dealings with the Samaritans." And later revealed he to Peter that the Gentiles were as acceptable as the Jews. "What God hath cleansed, that call not thou common." His was a way of teaching equalities the slow, free-agency way rather than by revolutionary force.

He was grieved with the class distinction as shown by the priest and Levite toward the man rescued by the good Samaritan, and poured forth his indictments against the many groups who dealt in such hypocrisies, but instead of revolutionary tactics, he tried to shame them into a change of their way of life.

He deplored the accumulation of great wealth at the expense of the downtrodden. . . . He made no effort to organize political forces to take from the rich, but taught correct principles of welfare in which the poor would be provided for by the rich voluntarily. . . .

Aren't you becoming an extremist and losing your balance somewhat, and in that very radicalism will you not bring to yourself impotency in the very results which you would attain? Wouldn't you far better align yourself with all the constructive forces which attempt in a slower, more peaceful way to reach the same ends? With your great ability you might be able to go far in spreading the message of good will through Church media.

May I say again: when you include in the gospel plan of Christ the family, there is nothing else in all the world worth bothering with. Everything else is incidental only. Assume that you become the world leader of Socialism and in it have marked success, but through your devotion to it you fail to live the gospel. Where are you then? Is anything worthwhile which will estrange you from your friends, your Church membership, your family, your eternal promises, your faith? You might say that such estrangement is not necessarily a result of your political views, but truthfully hasn't your overpowering interest in your present views already started driving a wedge? (*Teachings of Spencer W. Kimball,* pp. 408-409)

Ezra Taft Benson

The fifth and final principle that is basic to our understanding of the Constitution is that governments should have only limited powers. The important thing to keep in mind is that the people who have created their government can give to that government only such powers as they, themselves, have in the first place. Obviously, they cannot give that which they do not possess.

By deriving its just powers from the governed, government becomes primarily a mechanism for defense against bodily harm, theft, and involuntary servitude. It cannot claim the power to redistribute money or property nor to force reluctant citizens to perform acts of charity against their will. Government is created by the people. The creature cannot exceed the creator. (*Ensign,* Sept. 1987, p. 8)

Few men anywhere have written and taught so clearly of the evils of communism, socialism, and of an unelected, nonrepresentative world police and enforcing agency as the prophet the Lord raised up specifically for the very time that these evils were encroaching upon American society, Ezra Taft Benson. One fails to see only if he fails to open his eyes.

The Image, Mark, and Number of the Beast

Among the best known symbols in the Book of Revelation is the image, mark and number of the beast, a great sign of Satan's kingdom. All of the earth's commerce will be controlled by it; and everyone, small, great, rich, poor, free and bond, will receive a mark in their right hand or in their foreheads (Revelation 13:16). There may yet be further fulfillment of this prophecy, but let's look at what has happened so far. Is there such a type of this in the world today?

Consider the social security number. The author believes this number fits quite well in the framework of the prophecies of John, as well as with statements of modern-day prophets. The author will not be so bold as to state that the social security number is the mark of the beast, but the pieces seem to fit; and if it is not, at the very least it has had the effect of conditioning Americans to more readily accept such a mark when it is eventually offered. The author encourages the reader to consider the evidence which follows.

The purpose of the mark of the beast is to deceive them that dwell on earth (Revelation 13:14). David O. McKay teaches: "Free agency may well be a measuring rod by which the actions of men or organizations of nations may be judged" (*Secrets of a Happy Life,* pp. 152-154).

This is a truth that is profound, a precious key to measure the righteousness of any act. This truth is worth the mental effort required to internalize it in daily living. Everyone cherishes their ability and right to make choices. Wealth, for instance, is sought after because its accumulation extends the range of choice. Wealth is produced by labor, and this labor facilitates the ability to make choices. The problems with wealth come from how it is acquired (honest labor versus extortion); how it is regarded and used (trusted in or worshipped versus thankfully used and shared); and more important, how it is stored (hoarded versus cast upon the waters and laid up in heaven).

The scriptures contain several references to the phrase "labor or works of darkness" with respect to Satan, contrasted by the "labor and works of light" spoken of when referring to Christ. Both types of labor create choices, but the difference is seen when comparing the effect of the labor on free agency. To those who labor for Christ, knowledge is balanced by its righteous use, called wisdom. Wealth and power are balanced by the ability to use them to help rather than hurt others, called morality. Creation is balanced by beauty; justice is balanced by mercy. All are governed by the underlying principles of love and charity. This path leads the individual on until he or she becomes Christlike, and is eventually entrusted with "all things." In contrast, those who choose the works of darkness eventually find that their range of possible choices gets smaller and smaller. Metaphorically, this is the descent into the darkness, the confining and ever-narrowing sides of the bottomless pit. Individuals who choose this course often seek to make up for the loss in their choicemaking ability by unrighteously usurping power and position, thereby making choices which rightfully belong to others. They first covet, then steal, the wealth produced by labor; or worse, they rob others of the very rights of self-reliance, independence, and free agency.

These basic principles can protect people from the sinful condition of equating morality with legality, or the hypocrisy of being concerned only with outward observances. The critical question the author asks about the social security number is: does it enhance freedom, or take it away? Freedom comes through independence, and independence comes through the acceptance of responsibility. A major message of the gospel of Christ is that individuals are to take responsibility and become independent as people, groups, and nations, and thus proclaim liberty throughout the land.

King David was severely chastened for numbering the children of Israel (2 Samuel 24:1-24). It appears that there is a natural tendency for a government to begin to think of its people as possessions after they number them. This is exactly the opposite of the true order of government. The accompanying fourteen percent social security tax is fourteen percent of a person's working time that he has lost complete freedom over. The argument for the social security system sounds surprisingly like Satan's premortal argument for the system he wished to impose:

> And I, the Lord God, spake unto Moses, saying: That Satan, whom thou has commanded in the name of mine Only Begotten, is the same which was from the beginning, and he came before me, saying—Behold, here am I, send me, I will be thy son, and I will redeem all mankind, that one soul shall not be lost, and surely I will do it; wherefore give me thine honor.
>
> (Moses 4:1)

Satan's argument was "I will redeem all mankind [save them from their own stupidity, destruction, ineptness], that not one soul shall be lost [temporally or spiritually]. Surely, I will do it [or the government system I control]. Wherefore, give me thine honor [the place in government reserved for Christ or his agents]." Moses 4:3 continues: "Wherefore, because that Satan rebelled against me [constitutional government is based on the principle that it is immoral for government to take what belongs to one person and give it to another], and sought to destroy the agency of man [only a fourteen percent slavery on this tax issue], which I, the Lord, had given him [constitutional government was given by God by the raising up of righteous men for that very purpose]. . . . I caused that Satan should be cast down [destruction of those who worship the beast and carry his number]." Nevertheless, there may be a differentiation between those who worship the beast and those who are simply overcome by the beast (Revelation 13:7).

Social security—what is it? The prophets have plainly taught that socialism is of Satan. Security? That is what Satan has promised in return for free agency. Those who are forced to pay more into the system than they can get out are being robbed. Those who vote and support the use of government's forceful arm to unconstitutionally take that free agency away from their brothers and sisters are robbers, at least in their hearts. Chapter 18 of Ezra Taft Benson's excellent book, *An Enemy Hath Done This,* is entitled "Social Security, Fact and Fiction." President Benson's first words in this chapter are "Social security is unconstitutional." In the same book, President Benson quotes Benjamin Franklin as saying, "They that can give up essential liberty to obtain a little temporary safety, deserve neither liberty nor safety."

The author believes Gadianton the robber would be most pleased with the present social security system. Another excellent book on this subject is *The Great And Abominable Church of the Devil,* by the late H. Verlan Anderson, formerly of the First Quorum of Seventy. By deception, and in the sight of the beast, verse 14 goes on to say, "to them that dwell on the earth, that they should make an image to the beast . . . which had the wound by a sword, and did live." If the beast is communism, then the image of the beast (verse 15) most assuredly would have to be socialism.

Communism and socialism have identical goals. Only the tactics used to bring them about differ. Socialism creeps in by the voice and will of a deceived people. The "republic" discussed by this nation's forefathers, in which God is looked to for the supreme law of the land, is replaced by democracy, where God's law is replaced by man's vote. Communism espouses revolution and force as a means to achieving the same goals. Ezra Taft Benson taught this concept for many years. How many have ears to hear?

> The paths this nation is following, if moved forward thereon, will inevitably lead to socialism or communism, and these two are as like as two peas in a pod in their ultimate effect upon our liberties.
> Ezra Taft Benson, Conference Report, April 1963, p. 112

> And never forget for one moment that communism and socialism are state slavery.
> Ezra Taft Benson, Conference Report, April 1963, p. 111

> "Our real enemies," said President Clark, "are communism and its running mate, socialism."
> Ezra Taft Benson, Conference Report, April 1963, p. 111

> We should become informed about communism, about socialism, and about Americanism. What better way can one become informed than by first studying the inspired words of the prophets and using that as a foundation against which to test all other materials? This is in keeping with the Prophet Joseph Smith's motto, "When the Lord commands, do it."
> Teachings of Ezra Taft Benson, p. 305

> History proves that the growth of the welfare state is difficult to check before it comes to its full flower of dictatorship. But let us hope that this time around, the trend can be reversed. If not, then we will see the inevitability of complete socialism—probably within our lifetime.
> Ezra Taft Benson, Conference Report, October 1968, p. 21

Ezra Taft Benson has written an entire book titled *The Red Carpet, Socialism—the Royal Road to Communism.* This nation's social programs are the image of communism within the current government structure. Verse 15 says that not worshipping the beast *will become a life and death matter!*

Many people misunderstand or misquote verse 16. The word is in their right hand or *in* their foreheads. The mark is not *on,* but *in.* If someone asks a person for their social security number, he or she will either take their right hand and present them with a card ("in your hand,") or else will recall it from that portion (forehead) of their brain where numbers are stored.

Verse 17 states that "no man might buy or sell, save he that had the mark, or the name of the beast, or the number of his name." This sounds like a tremendous invasion of a person's freedom. Surely Americans would never accept such an encroachment—or would we? What is the major commodity that most people sell? Their labor. Try to get or keep most jobs without a social security number. How do most people buy and sell? Through banks. Again, try to open a banking account without a social security number, or try to get a bank card, or even make a major purchase, such as a house, without a social security number. The author refrains from calling this system "socialist" security.

Verse 17 also states that this number is the number of his name. In the military, in schools, on many driver's licenses, and on the rolls of government, the social security number is an exact replacement of a person's name. Verse 18 states that it is the number of a man. This could be another way of saying that it is a man's number. What is your number? Of course, your social security number.

The whole concept of the mark of the beast must be very important, since it is mentioned six times in John's Revelation (Revelation 13:16, 17; 14:11; 15:2; 16:2; 19:20; 20:4). In the search for understanding, one must go back to the original Greek. The word for mark is translated from the Greek word charagma. In this context the meaning of the word would be a brand, tattoo, or stamp as a badge of servitude. (*Strong's Exhaustive Concordance of the Bible,* p. 5480 in the Greek Testament). Slaves have security, but it is in trade for their freedom. By branding a slave, their freedom can be strictly controlled, their movement monitored, and their privileges metered. There will surely be those who will accept the mark unawares. Just as the Amlicites marked themselves, so shall it follow in the last days.

> Now the Amlicites knew not that they were fulfilling the words of God when they began to mark themselves in their foreheads; nevertheless they had come out in open rebellion against God; therefore it was expedient that the curse should fall upon them.
>
> (Alma 3:18)

The mark of the beast may evolve. It could begin as a small amount of additional security traded for a correspondingly small amount of freedom, either one's own, or worse yet, extracted from a neighbor by the forceful arm of government. As the nation slips into socialism, the costs and the controls also increase.

A last observation: verse 15 states "that he had power to give life unto the image of the beast . . . and should speak." The social security issue was the first issue to gain popular support and launch this nation on its rapid slip into the welfare state. It was this issue that helped the citizens of this nation begin thinking and speaking like the socialists we have become. There may yet come a time of completely black and white contrasts, a time when the identification number is no longer held voluntarily in the hand or mind, but is a mandatory instrument of control. In such a choice, choosing and being branded as "owned by the image of the beast" means rejecting Christ and being rejected by him.

A Possible Fulfillment of the Mark

The author recently adopted a wild horse from the Bureau of Land Management. Instead of a brand, the horse had been injected with a microscopic chip under its skin. Could such a high tech branding be a precursor of what is intended for all?

An outspoken teacher on this subject is Dr. Carl Sanders. According to Dr. Sanders' testimony, he was the chief engineer leading a team of a hundred people in the original research to develop this technology. Their assignment was to develop biotechnical solutions for medical problems. They successfully used microchip technology to help a young lady who had severed her spine in an accident. Through the use of a microchip, she regained the use of, though not the feeling in, her legs. They refined this to a 7 mm long, .75 mm in diameter microchip and combined it with a transmitter that put out a signal that could be picked up on a L-band satellite. As they began to experiment in its various uses, they determined that implanting it surgically was not efficient, and worked until it was small enough to be injected with a hypodermic needle. A group called "InfoPet," in Los Angles, currently claims they can monitor the whereabouts of a pet, once tagged, to within ten feet of its location. Dr. Sanders says it is also being used to monitor the location of Alzheimer's patients, and over 17,000 babies have received it.

It was not until several years after helping develop this technology that Dr. Sanders became a converted Christian. As he read in the Book of Revelation, he came across, for the first time, Revelation 13:16. He immediately questioned whether the device he had helped develop could be used in the fulfillment of this prophecy. He tells how "the Spirit said to me, 'Look up the word *Mark*.'" He argued for a minute with this prompting, until it came again, this time stronger: "Look up the word *Mark* in the Greek!" He used the *Strong's Concordance* and discovered the word *charagma:* a scratch or etching, as a badge of servitude, or an engraving in the skin, like a tattoo. Then the spirit directed him to look up the word six hundred and sixty-six. He brushed that prompting aside, reasoning that it wasn't a word, but a number. The prompting came again. He complied. He found, indeed, that in the original Greek, six hundred three score and six appears as a word. The root of the word was *steizo,* to stick; a mark incised or punched into for mark of ownership. He says of this experience: "I read it, and I wept. And I asked God to forgive me. And now I've asked man to forgive me for the part I played in this."

Another discovery of the Greek roots to these words revealed the meaning: "an engraving, an exact copy or an express image." The microchip described by Dr. Sanders has the capability of storing a digitized readout of a person's photograph, thumbprint, social security number, and physical description. Though most think of a thumbprint as an engraving, the government term for engraving is "express image," according to Dr. Sanders. It also can hold the same information as today's "Smart Card" (which is being used in some states, such as Maryland, to prevent welfare fraud): a person's address, family history, criminal record, and IRS history. All of this is in a microchip small enough to be inserted with a hypodermic needle!

In their research and development of this technology, Dr. Sander's team had to solve the problem of how to recharge the battery that powers the chip. Many on the team were determined to use a lithium battery, and though Dr. Sanders disagreed and tried to steer them toward other sources, they did end up using lithium as a source. This battery depends on changes in body temperature for recharging. The team spent nearly two million dollars researching the places on the body that experience the most change in temperature to decide the best place to insert the microchip. Scientifically, they arrived at the two best locations: on the forehead, one and a half inches below the hairline, and on the back of the right hand. In Revelation 16:2, the Lord tells John that when the vials are poured out, those who have the mark of the beast will have a grievous sore (not break out in sores, just one sore). When Dr. Sanders read this, he went to the doctors at the Boston Medical Center who had worked on this project with him. He asked one, "What happens to the person with the microchip implant if there was a blow struck, and it were to break?" The doctor said, "Well, he'd get a sore." When pressed again for any other medical insights into this, he replied in exasperation, "He'd get a sore that wouldn't heal, Carl. HE'D HAVE A GRIEVOUS SORE!" Dr. Sanders was amazed that this man, an atheist, would utter the exact words of John's prophecy.

Dr. Sanders is concerned about the potential of the electronic media to be used in a way that would take away freedom. The 1986 Emigration Control Act gave the President of the United States power to authorize any means to identify the population, and this device is perfectly suited for that use. Dr. Sanders now spends his time in testimony against the spiritual and physical dangers of accepting such a mark. Here is Dr. Carl Sanders message to all the Christian Church today:

> God is omnipotent and omnipresent, but the AntiChrist has to use every bit of technology he can to keep track of us, and that is the reason we've come to this. It's not an easy message; it is a hard message to give. But God is on the throne, and we win, and if you check the tomb, it's empty! We are living in the most exciting time we could live in. The reason we need to pull together as a body of Christ is to support one another, to help one another, to lift one another up! I'm sharing with you a message: the technology is here.
>
> We now have 20 or 30 satellites overhead that can read a postage stamp laying on a tennis court. The satellite can read your license plate every 19 minutes without any problem at all.
>
> The new LEO (Low Earth Orbiting) satellites have just gone up. They are orbiting 98 to 100 miles up, 66 of them being put up by Motorola in conjunction with the Russians. These satellites will do away with all cellular towers, and there will not be a place where you can go to hide. We can pick up your body temperature change right now; the difference between 98.6 and 104. Now don't get in despair on me, because I'm telling you again, WE WIN. Jesus was standing there, they picked up stones to stone him, and he walked right through their midst, and they saw him not. We need to understand where we are walking when we walk with him.
>
> First Thessalonians 5:1-11 reads: "But of the times and seasons, brethren, ye have no need. For yourselves know perfectly that the day of the Lord cometh as a thief in the night. For when they [folks, there are still 27,000 warheads pointed in this direction, and we have disarmed 65% of our silos!] shall say peace and safety, then sudden destruction cometh upon them as travail upon a woman with child, and they shall not escape. But ye, brethren, are not in darkness that day should overtake you as a thief. Ye are all the children of light, and the children of the day: we are not of the night, nor of darkness. Therefore let us not sleep,

as do others; but let us watch and be sober. . . . Wherefore comfort yourselves together, and edify one another.

(Preparedness Fair Expo '93)

Further information from Dr. Sanders, including tapes and literature, is available at Trumpet Ministries, 510 Main Street, Cottage Grove, OR 97424.

Understanding the Number of the Beast

In seeking to understand the number of the beast, six hundred three score and six, it is necessary to return to the original Greek. The following is taken from the Greek Dictionary of the New Testament portion of *Strong's Concordance,* by James Strong, S.T.D. L.L.D p. 78.

> 5516. χξϛ **chi xi stigma,** *khee xee stig'-ma;* the 22d, 14th and an obsol. letter (*4742* as a *cross*) of the Greek alphabet (intermediate between the 5th and 6th), used as numbers; denoting respectively 600, 60 and 6; 666 as a numeral:—six hundred threescore and six.

A recently published book entitled *Written by the Finger of God,* by Joe Sampson, illuminates several techniques used by Hebrew rabbis and scholars to encode, or hide, treasures of truth within the framework of Hebrew writing. These ancient techniques are also found in the writings of many Book of Mormon prophets, and also in the revelations from Jesus Christ to Joseph Smith in the Doctrine and Covenants. One of these techniques is called *notarikon.*

> Notarikon is the concept that each individual letter of the Hebrew language has a meaning, definition, power or force in and of itself before words are created. This technique allows the Rabbi to dissect any word into its component parts or separate portions of words to discover hidden meanings in each part.
> The classic example of this technique is the dissection of the word "truth." The word truth, written in the block form, is written with three letters. The Rabbinical tradition is that these letters refer to the concepts of past, present, and future. In D & C 93, Jesus supplies the prophet Joseph with the same definition: "Truth is knowledge of things as they are, were, and as they are to come."

(*Written by the Finger of God,* p. 29)

Notarikon, then, is the search for the meaning of words by combining or studying the meaning given to the individual letters. Often the shape of the letters themselves holds the key to their meaning. The number six hundred and sixty-six is spelled with only three Greek letters. If one were reading this number spelled as a word in Greek, he would see three images. The first is the fallen, or sideways, cross. The second is a serpent, and the third looks like a number 5. This letter in Greek is pronounced *stigma*. In Greek, *stigma* is not only a letter, but as a word it has a specific meaning. A *stigma* is a tattoo mark. The word has its root from the meaning "to stick," as in the sticking that takes place to put ink under the skin to create the tattoo. In modern English, the word *stigma* means a mark of disgrace or infamy; a stain or reproach, as on one's reputation. Thus the number 666 contains symbolic images that show the mark to be a label of the anti-Christ, probably placed under the skin.

Additional information can be obtained by using notarikon technique and looking at 666 as a number, not just as a word. In notarikon the number six (taken from the sixth letter in the Hebrew alphabet) is the nail, symbolic of a covenant promise, the divine decree, that which cannot be broken, removed, and the unbreakable law. The Greeks and Hebrews, in their fascination with numbers, assigned characteristics and qualities to numbers based on how the number functioned mathematically. The number six is described as the first "perfect" number, because all of its factors add up to equal itself (*Greek Mathematical Philosophy*, p. 21). The sixth day of the year also has special significance to Christ. According to the Nephite record, the resurrection occurred on the sixth day of the first month of their calendar (3 Nephi 8:5, 23). April 6 is also the day chosen by Christ to restore his Church. D & C 20:1 also seems to indicate that April 6 coincides with the anniversary of Christ's birth. Putting these concepts together, 6 gives a representation of Christ and his earthly ministry.

The Hebrews also used a concept known as TRSQ. (In Hebrew writing, the vowels are supplied from the mind of the reader.) The name of this method is taken from the last four letters of the Hebrew alphabet, spelled backwards. This word, TRSQ, means that if one takes a word and mirrors the spelling, it creates a new word with exactly the opposite meaning as the original word. It is little wonder, then, that when the number 6 is reversed to 9, it creates the symbol for the serpent (again taken from the 9th letter in the Hebrew alphabet). The number 9 is also symbolic of ripeness in Arabic numerals: after 9, the numbers start the sequence over with 10. Notarikon technique will often yield the meaning for letters by their shape. Nine (9) is the number with the big head; it contains the element of pride. This is reminiscent of Satan's premortal boast that he would save mankind his way and take all the glory unto himself.

One method with a history of ancient use was to reduce multi-digit numbers to a single digit for purpose of analysis. The process was to add the digits together and repeat the process until a single digit is obtained. Thus 666 equals $6 + 6 + 6 = 18$; $1 + 8 = 9$. Using this process, 666 is really the serpent masquerading as the Savior. Another interesting mathematical feature of the number 9 is that by using the above equation, any single digit number that is combined with number 9 is forever damned (ends up where it started, without progression) to repeat the process. Example: $5 + 9 = 14$; $1 + 4 = 5$. The number nine is the epitome of the concept of forever learning, but never coming to a knowledge of the truth.

The number 666 is obviously some type of code, and since this method of analysis predates John, it may have merit.

America Has Strayed From the Constitution

Americans today are just as apostate from the principles of the divinely inspired Constitution as the misguided among the Jews at the time of Christ were from the priesthood principles of the gospel!

The teachings of this chapter appear centrally in the revelation given by John, and also appear to be central to understanding the message the revelation was meant to convey. This part of the book was approached with much prayer, meditation, and thought on the part of the author, knowing beforehand that much of that which the author feels needs to be said may be extremely unpopular. In looking at the scarlet beast as communism, the author originally felt the burden of carrying a unique interpretation, but later learned that many have come to this conclusion independently. In reading Bruce R. McConkie's *Doctrinal New Testament Commentary,* Volume 3, the author was pleased to see the interpretation of the beast offered as a question: "They worshipped the beast. Even the kingdoms, which follows Satan's course, shall inspire awe, reverence, and worship on the part of Godless men. In this connection, here is a point to ponder: Do those who espouse Godless communism substitute the worship of the state for the worship of God?" (*Doctrinal New Testament Commentary,* Vol. 3, p. 522). No other possible explanation was offered by Elder McConkie.

This is only the very beginning of interpretation, however, for if these concepts are what John prophecied, it proscribes the need to carry them through to the interrelations between the other entities John describes. The exactness and precision with which the author's understanding of world politics matches John's description, here given, is a testimony to the author of the validity of his research.

When the first draft of this book was completed, the author had simply skipped past the mark and number of the beast with the notation that it was a concept not currently understood. The author was familiar with many of the interpretations being put forth, but was uncomfortable using any of them. When the thought was entertained that perhaps this symbolism was related to the social security number, the thought was automatically dismissed. It proved to be, however, one of those thoughts that just seemed impossible to cast away. Finally, the author did open his mind to this possibility, to see how this concept would fit. What followed felt almost as a whirlwind of inspiration. It seemed almost impossible to write fast enough to capture the concepts that were flowing. What was written was almost exactly as it now appears in this chapter.

Looking at "666" as a code was also a new concept and experience for the author. Having recently read, studied, and been amazed at Joe Sampson's book, *Written by the Finger of God,* and also being lucky enough to have recently moved close to Mr. Sampson's home, and now counting him as a close personal friend and mentor, it was only natural to apply the techniques of his book to this task. Again, the pieces fit. The application of ancient Greek mathematical concepts was accomplished through the author's own research, but again, the sources seemed to jump out and beg to be looked at. The reader is challenged to carefully consider the possible interpretations given in this book. If they are rejected, the challenge remains to find other explanations which match the criteria given by John.

14
The Harvesting of the Earth

Once again, a dramatic shift can be sensed in John's writing. This book truly is a book of contrasts—salvation versus destruction, righteousness versus wickedness, freedom versus bondage, Christ versus Satan. It is as if, in these last days, both Christ and Satan give each individual the fullness of opportunity to see who they will follow, and how far.

In verse 1, John looks and sees a lamb standing on mount Sion. With him are 144,000, having his Father's name written in their foreheads. This calling up to mount Sion is related, at least in type, to the Zion of Enoch's day, which was called up.

> And the Lord said: Blessed is he through whose seed Messiah shall come; for he saith—I am Messiah, the king of Zion, the Rock of Heaven, which is broad as eternity; whoso cometh in at the gate and climbeth up by me shall never fall; wherefore, blessed are they of whom I have spoken, for they shall come forth with songs of everlasting joy.
> (Moses 7:53)

These are able to sing "as it were a new song before the throne" (Revelation 14:3). This blessing is endowed only upon the 144,000.

Verses 4 and 5 indicate the special qualifications of this priesthood body. One, they have not partaken of sexual sin. Two, they are totally loyal and obedient to Christ. They follow him whithersoever he goes. Three, their mouths have no guile. To be guileless means to be sincere, honest, straightforward and frank. The association with the mouth means that what they speak and teach is in total harmony with how they act and live. This truly is a characteristic to set men apart.

Following this song are the voices of seven angels, giving a perspective from the righteous. The *First angel* brings the gospel to them that dwell on earth. The reader is told to fear God, give glory, prepare for judgment, and worship the Creator.

The *Second angel* announces the fall of Babylon, the great city. The reason given for her fall is that she forced all nations to drink of the wine of the wrath of her fornication.

The *Third angel* warns that if any man worships the beast and his image, and receives his mark in his forehead or his hand, the same shall suffer the wrath of God. This wrath, indignation, torment, fire and brimstone will be felt while the person is in the presence of the holy angels, and the presence of the Lamb. Evidently Christ and his angels are there waiting and hoping to be called upon. The same promise Christ gave to the ancient church is held out to latter-day saints:

> Behold, I stand at the door, and knock; if any man hear my voice, and open the door, I will come in to him, and will sup with him, and he with me.
> To him that overcometh will I grant to sit with me in my throne, even as I also overcame, and am set down with my Father in his throne.
> (Revelation 3:20-21)

John tied together two sins that bring the wrath of God. First is the idolatry of worshipping the beast. The author believes it is a specific warning against the religion of Satan as taught by Karl Marx, the beast being communism, and the image of the beast being socialism:

> For communism is just another form of socialism, as is fascism. So now you can see the picture. These liberals want you to know how much they are doing for you—with your tax money, of course. But they don't want you to realize that the path they are pursuing is socialistic and that socialism is the same as communism in its ultimate effect on our liberties. When you point this out they want to shut you up; they accuse you of maligning them, of casting aspersions, of being political. No matter whether they label their bottle as liberalism, progressivism, or social reform, I know the contents of the bottle is poison to this Republic and I'm going to call it poison.
> (*An Enemy Hath Done This*, p. 43)

The second sin is the receiving of the mark of the beast. Once again, there may be a distinction between those who worship the beast and receive his mark, and those who are overcome by the beast. Under careful scrutiny, one can see that the attacks, directed at the messenger, are a Satanic ploy to divert attention from the message.

Verse 12 reads: "Here is the patience of the saints." As shown earlier, there will be a short period of time when the beast shall overcome the saints. Even those that keep the commandments of God will be tried (Revelation 14:12).

THE HARVESTING OF THE EARTH

There are saints who yet have work to do, or yet need trials to build characters worthy of living with Christ.

A similar condition is seen in Mosiah 24. The people of Alma had been wicked, but had repented. Despite this repentance, they were called upon to suffer for a short period, even as they lived in righteousness. Before their miraculous delivery, they received this promise and blessing:

> And now it came to pass that the burdens which were laid upon Alma and his brethren were made light; yea, the Lord did strengthen them that they could bear up their burdens with ease, and they did submit cheerfully and with patience to all the will of the Lord.
> And it came to pass that so great was their faith and their patience that the voice of the Lord came unto them again, saying: Be of good comfort, for on the morrow I will deliver you out of bondage.
> (Mosiah 24:15-16)

Among those who will endure this affliction is a group of righteous who will actually suffer death. The Lord has a very special blessing awaiting these:

> And I heard a voice from heaven saying unto me, Write, Blessed are the dead which die in the Lord from henceforth: Yea, saith the Spirit, that they may rest from their labours; and their works do follow them.
> (Revelation 14:13)

At this time comes the harvesting of the earth. Four people will lead this work. The first is Christ. He is pictured on a cloud, symbolic of a place high above the earth, where he is fully aware of all the doings in his kingdom. He has a golden crown upon his head, symbolic of divine authority to do this work. He carries a sharp sickle as a tool to accomplish this work.

The second and third angels come out of the temple in heaven. They also carry instruments of harvest. The description of the third may give a clue to who these angels could be. This angel comes out from the altar, a place of sacrifice and covenant making. This earth is the place of sacrifice. Could this be a reuniting of the First Presidency (Peter, James, and John) under Christ? According to D & C 7:6-7 John will be as a flaming fire and a ministering angel to those who shall be heirs of salvation on earth. He is to be a minister for Peter and James, and to these three are the power and keys given until Christ shall come.

At this point it may be useful to again examine the last-days mission of John. Not only is it John's mission to write and testify of the important events of the last days, giving those who would listen great hope and strength in the face of tremendous adversity, but John is also commissioned to be a key participator in the Lord's work of the last days. From Revelation 10 and D & C & C 77:14 it can be seen that John was given a mission that was sweet and bitter at the end of time, when Satan will be bound. This mission included the gathering of the Tribes of Israel. Here he is called Elias, coming to restore all things (D & C 77:1). This calling of Elias contains a cross-reference to D & C 77:9 (see also LDS Bible Dictionary). It shows that John is also the angel described in Revelation 7:2-3. He is the one who gives the seal of the living God to the 144,000 and others called up with them. The final destruction, or reaping of the earth, is delayed until this is accomplished. In Revelation 14, two angels from the temple of God in heaven unite their voices with the voice of an angel upon the altar, or earth (author's interpretation), saying it is time for the final reaping, even the great winepress of the wrath of God. Their voices go up to the Son of man, who sits on the cloud, sickle in hand. Perhaps John is a type of a last days' Enoch, to separate the wheat from the tares and call down the reapers from heaven.

If understood fully, the Book of Revelation itself is a great sifter of people. Through this study one can see and know, in black and white, the works of Christ and Satan. Chapters 10 and 7 show that this work of gathering is accomplished in days, not instantly (See also Moses 7:27). In other words, it may be up to today's saints to decide when they have had enough suffering. At what point does one decide to give up the yoke of Satan and take upon himself the yoke of Christ?

> Take my yoke upon you, and learn of me; for I am meek and lowly in heart: and ye shall find rest unto your souls.
> For my yoke is easy, and my burden is light.
> (Matthew 11:29-30)

Verses 19 and 20 show that the harvest is accomplished. It is likened unto treading the winepress of the wrath of God.

15
Victory Over Plagues for the Righteous

Chapters 15 and 16 of Revelation give greater insight into the plagues of the last days. As John introduces chapter 15, he once again shows the seven angels with their plagues. To help give perspective, he also gives another view of the celestial world. Joseph Smith explained that this earth, when it belongs to Christ in its sanctified, immortal state, will be "like unto crystal and will be a Urim and Thummim to the inhabitants who dwell thereon, whereby all things pertaining to an inferior kingdom . . . will be made manifest to those who dwell on it" (D & C 130:9). The glorified and perfected earth is seen as a sea of glass. Those exalted saints who reside there have achieved victory over the beast, and over his mark, and over the number of his name (or Satan). They are endowed to sing the song of Moses and of Christ.

The words "to a song of Moses" are recorded in Exodus 15. The song speaks of the horse and his rider being thrown into the sea. If the same imagery could be used as John used in Revelation 6 to describe the seals, then the horse spoken of has to do with conquering, removal of peace from the earth, judgments, and death followed by hell. This would certainly be a fitting start for a song of Christ, because he has overcome all of these. The song was sung right after the deliverance of the children of Israel from the armies of Pharaoh. Likewise, in latter days the song is sung again after the defeat of the enemies of Christ. The first part of the song is a war song, followed by the gathering, dwelling and inheritance of the Lord's people. The song concludes with the promise that the Lord shall reign forever and ever.

The Coming of Two Cities from Heaven

In verse 5 the temple of the tabernacle of the testimony in heaven is opened. As already noted, this relates to the coming of Enoch's Zion (see chapter 11 of this book) and the fact that there will be two millennial centers of Zion. Joseph Smith taught that the whole of the Americas is designated as Zion, a land of promise, and that the New Jerusalem will be located here (10th Article of Faith). Old Jerusalem, the Holy Land, also has promises, covenants and blessings prophesied. Micah 4:2 teaches that the law shall go forth from Zion, and the word of the Lord from Jerusalem. The millennial world is to have two great centers.

The author concludes from this that the land of Palestine, where Christ emphasized the gospel during his earthly ministry, will be held accountable for that portion, and continue that work into the millennium. In America, constitutional law and government was given by Christ through the raising up of righteous men for that very purpose. Those who inherited that legacy will be held accountable to return it back to Christ (Micah 4:2). Historically, there have been overlaps or reversals of these roles. Joseph (whose seed was to inherit the Americas) was also blessed to be a spiritual teacher to his brothers (the sons of Israel). This was in addition to his governmental role. The right of kingship comes through the lineage of Judah (whose seed remains in Palestine), to Christ.

It appears from Micah 4:2 and Isaiah 2:3 that Christ will continue to send forth his law portion of the gospel from the Americas. To the Americas, the tabernacle from heaven returning to earth will be Enoch's city of Zion. To the land of Palestine, the tabernacle from heaven will be Melchizedek's city of Salem. (The name *Jerusalem* means *New Salem*.) This accounts for the thunders, lightnings, voices from heaven, and a great earthquake in both places (Revelation 6:12, 8:5, 11:19, 16:18).

The cities of Enoch and Salem were of the same order. They were both translated through righteousness. Compare JST Genesis 9:21 with JST Genesis 14:33, 34 (pages 797 and 798 in the Appendix of the LDS edition of the Bible). There are interesting similarities between righteous Noah, who was chosen to remain on earth to bless and reseed the earth and to carry on the gospel, and Abraham. Abraham knew Melchizedek and was fully aware of the great work of repentance being wrought among that formerly wicked people. Abraham was chosen to remain on earth to bless the earth with his seed, carry forth the gospel, and preserve the record. Ever after, Abraham was known as a stranger on earth (Genesis 23:4).

Jacob and the City of Salem

This perspective sheds a whole new light on the story of Jacob. It can be assumed that Jacob had the record, or had been told by his grandfather, Abraham, of Enoch's city, or had a similar record from Melchizedek's city of Salem. He would have been aware that even after the city was caught up, angels came down, supposedly from that city, to catch up many by the powers of heaven into Zion (See Moses 7:27). He would have also known that a blessing was pronounced upon those who came up to the Rock of Heaven and climbed up by way of Jehovah, thus entering Zion (Moses 7:53).

Jacob went to a place named Bethel, translated as "House of God" (Genesis 28:19). Jacob was there because he had brought on the displeasure of his father Isaac by his deception, and because his brother Esau was seeking his life. He has been sent to ask his Uncle Laban for a wife. At such a lonely time, it would seem natural that a man of his understanding would wish to go to the place where Salem had been, hoping to be caught up to the city of peace. In the language of today, he might have said, "Beam me up. It's really rough down here."

It is at this very place that Jacob saw, in a dream, a ladder from earth reaching the heavens (Genesis 28:12). Jacob saw the Lord standing above (28:13). The Lord gave Jacob the promise of his spirit, protection, the land, and numerous seed that would bless all the families of the earth. This was a repeat of Abraham's promise (28:15). Jacob said this about the place:

> And he was afraid, and said, How dreadful is this place! this is none other but the house of God, and this is the gate of heaven.
> (Genesis 28:17)

The next time Jacob saw heavenly beings was just before returning to face his brother Esau. He had learned that Esau was coming to meet him with an army of four hundred men. Once again, he retreated to Bethel (Genesis 32:1, 2; also Genesis 35:1). Jacob saw what he called "God's hosts." What followed must have been an interesting scene. This prophet of God grabbed hold of a heavenly being, whom he wrestled with all night. He says, "I will not let thee go, except thou bless me" (Genesis 32:26). Could Jacob be trying to be caught up again? He might have been saying to the angel, "I know where you are from. . . . If I just hang on long enough, will you take me with you?"

The last time Jacob had been to Bethel, he had been fleeing for his life from the Canaanites. The sacredness of this spot, named "House of God," is evidenced as Jacob was commanded to build an altar, to put away strange gods, to be clean and to change his garments. He was then again given a new name, "Israel." Notice what Jacob did at this place! This earthly, holy ground was a connecting link with the heavenly temple and the city of Salem. This parallels the earthly temples of today. Jacob's most important mission was upon earth. His trials had been necessary for his growth and the legacy of blessings his decendants now inherit. Like Jacob, one may face an earthly mission with reluctance. Though desiring the peace of Zion, one must remember that it was only after the people of Enoch and the city of Salem built Zion on earth that they enjoyed the privilege in heaven. Note that it was out of a wicked day, similar to the world of today, that this miraculous work was wrought.

There will be a reckoning for both the word and the law. Events of John's record might appear from the Jerusalem or American perspective, or more likely, very similarly from both. The Apostle John chose to tarry in the land of Palestine, and similarly, three disciples chose to tarry and carry on a latter-day work in the land of America. The events on the whole earth during the last days are great and dreadful, but more especially for the people of the Americas and the land of Palestine.

Returning to chapter 15, verse 8, it is seen that no man was able to enter that temple until the seven plagues were fulfilled. There could be two periods during which the righteous will be allowed to enter this temple of testimony in heaven: the first, when it is opened, and the second, after the purifying caused by the seven plagues.

16
Destruction and Plagues for the Wicked

Chapter 15 saw the pouring out of plagues, followed by a vision of the righteous who have overcome the beast. In chapter 16, a plague comes upon those who bear the mark of the beast, and upon them who worship his image. Again, the author believes that the beast is communism and the image of the beast is socialism. Notice that the plague is on those who have the mark and worship his image, tying the two sins together.

Verse 5 declares that God's judgments are just, and verse 6 declares that the wicked have shed the blood of the saints and the prophets. In God's perfect justice, the bloodthirsty wicked are given blood to drink. The fifth angel then pours out his vial, bringing tremendous destruction upon the seat of the beast.

In this chapter of the Book of Revelation, the plagues closely follow the format of those given in chapters 8 and 9. There are some differences, however. Chapter 16 is written from the perspective of what happens to the wicked followers and supporters of the beast (verses 8 and 9). The third angel, in chapter 8, seems to describe a landbased nuclear exchange, while here, in chapter 16, very similar plagues are depicted coming with the fourth and then the fifth angel as the vial of God's wrath is poured out upon the seat of the beast. This delay would be consistent with the retaliation after the first strike, as seen in the delayed response to Pearl Harbor in World War II.

John teaches that this plague is caused by a vial poured out upon the sun and power is given to scorch men with fire and great heat (Revelation 16:8-9). The hydrogen bomb came as a result of scientific theories about the production of helium from hydrogen in the sun. Through imitating the nuclear reactions on the sun, man has brought the sun's burning to the earth. The metaphor John chose could very well describe the hydrogen bomb. This also cross-references with the author's evidence and conclusions as discussed in chapter 8. An in-depth treatment of the subject is found in the book, *Superbombs, Saints and Scriptures*, Carl H. Jacob, SLC: Deseret Book, 1960.

The *sixth angel* pours out his vial on the great river Euphrates, so that it dries up and thus prepares the way for the kings of the East (cross-referenced to chapter 9:14). This scripture is vague without the historical knowledge that the Euphrates was the natural boundary between kingdoms in the days of the patriarchs. The Babylonians, Egyptians, Hittites, Assyrians and Mitanni people all, at some time, used the Euphrates River to define their boundaries. Drying up the river to prepare the way of the Kings could mean that boundaries are to be broken down. Broken borders would facilitate the combination of forces, making it possible to gather an army of two hundred million men, as described in the battle that follows in chapter 9.

John explains how the boundaries are broken. Three unclean spirits, like frogs, come out of the mouth of the dragon, or Satan. Second, they come out of the mouth of the beast, or communism. Third, they come out of the mouth of the false prophet. This division of Satanic power comes out of all three entities. The beast and the dragon have been named, but the false prophet has yet to be identified; yet historical considerations help with the selection of an appropriate candidate.

Possible Identity of the False Prophet

Joseph Smith is the prophet of the restoration. The knowledge, blessings, keys and organization of the Church were all restored during the administration of Joseph Smith, the prophet. Logic might lead one to expect that a great Satanic counterfeit would be established near the same time. Joseph Smith and Karl Marx were contemporaries. Both became leaders of great latter-day movements, which began in obscurity and now have worldwide influence: Joseph's, one of blessing, lifting, teaching and equality of the followers; and Karl's, one of death, misery and suffering, permitting no equality. Does anyone else so fully measure up to the expectations of the Satanic false prophet described? David O. McKay said:

> The entire concept and philosophy of Communism is diametrically opposed to everything for which the Church stands . . . Communism destroys man's God-given free agency. No member of this Church can be true to his faith, nor can any American be loyal to his trust, while lending aid, encouragement, or sympathy to any of these false philosophies; for if he does, they will prove snares to his feet.
>
> (*Improvement Era*, June 1966, pp. 477, 580)

The Works of Unclean Spirits

Verse 14 states that the unclean spirits are the spirits of devils. Their work seems miraculous. They go forth under the kings or world leaders, and as a result, the whole world is gathered to the battle of the great day of God Almighty. There is in the world today an organization that works with world leaders, has a socialistic agenda, is secretive by nature, and has the specific goal of removing national boundaries to create a new world order. Its members call themselves "trilateralists." The name "trilateralists" has to do with the areas of Europe, the Pacific Rim (including Asia), and the Americas. Senator Barry Goldwater gave this warning:

> This may cost me everything that I have, but I've got to get out and alert the American People. The Trilateral Commission represents a skillfully coordinated effort to seize control and consolidate the four centers of power, political, monetary, intellectual, and ECCLESIASTICAL. What the Trilateralists intend is the creation of a world-wide economic power superior to the government of the nation states. In other words, what they are driving, orchestrating, meshing, and gearing to accomplish is the New World Order, the one-world government.
>
> What the Trilateralists truly intend is the creation of a worldwide economic (money-banking) power superior to the political government of the nation-states involved. As managers and creators of the system THEY WILL RULE THE WORLD.
>
> (*With No Apologies,* p. 299)

A blessing is then pronounced upon those who are watching and are aware of these things, and on those who keep their garments (verse 15). This allusion to keeping covenants is a reminder that the time of the Lord's coming is unknown, and when he comes, the secret acts and thoughts of men will be revealed and shouted from the housetops. John then describes shame and embarrassment to be felt by those who have undertaken to cover their sins.

With the preparations done, the gathering of the wicked against the righteous is in a place called Armageddon. The seventh angel pours out his vial into the air. A great voice comes out of the temple in heaven (Enoch's Zion or Melchizedek's Salem, or probably both), saying, "It is done." From here come voices, and thunders, and lightnings and the greatest earthquake the world has ever known. Such a display could be expected as this magnificent city returns to earth from heaven. From a righteous perspective, this event will be truly great (Moses 7:62-63) and truly terrible for the wicked, for the destroyers become the destroyed.

The metaphorical great city, or Babylon, is divided into three parts. "And the cities of nations fell" (Revelation 16:19). This could be another way of saying that Satan's kingdom is divided three ways, with cities no longer holding national allegiance. Leaders promoting the New World Order have declared that their agenda or mission is to work through three areas to bring about their final goals:

1. *Economic,* through monopolized, centralized banking. This is in the spirit of Satan's teaching that one can buy anything in this world with money, including the souls of men.
2. *Political,* through the United Nations and amassing military power under this entity. This gives Satan the ability to take away man's agency, which the Lord had given man, and to use force to rule with blood and horror on this earth.
3. *Spiritual,* through the promotion of the new-age religion.

For a well-documented, up-to-date study of the Trilateral Commission and its closely associated counterpart, The Council on Foreign Relations, the author recommends *The Shadows of Power.* This book reveals the behind-the-scenes manipulation towards consolidation of power (economic, political, and spiritual), pursuant to the goal of a one-world government (a new world order).

The Prophet David O. McKay put it this way:

> Satan is making war against all the wisdom that has come to men through their ages of experience. He is seeking to overturn and destroy the very foundations upon which society, government, and religion rest. He aims to have men adopt theories and practices which he induced their forefathers, over the ages, to adopt and try, only to be discarded by them when found unsound, impractical, and ruinous. He plans to destroy liberty and freedom—*economic, political, and religious*—and set up in place thereof the greatest, most widespread, and most complete tyranny that has ever oppressed men. He is working under such perfect disguise that many do not recognize either him or his methods. There is no crime he would not commit, no debauchery he would not set up, no plague he would not send, no heart he would not break, no life he would not take, no soul he would not destroy. He comes as a thief in the night; he is a wolf in sheep's clothing. Without their knowing it,

the people are being urged down paths that lead only to destruction. Satan never before had so firm a grip on this generation as he has now.
(*Statements on Communism and the Constitution*)

Babylon now faces its judgment. Islands flee, mountains vanish, a great hail with ninety pound stones* comes out of heaven. The punishment for the ancient law of adultery is stoning; a scriptural metaphor often used for apostasy from the gospel of Christ is adultery. Apostasy is a spiritual equivalent to adultery. This plague figuratively and literally stones the unrepentant. The wicked still blaspheme God even as they suffer because of this great plague.

---

* Revelation 16:21 states that the great hail had stones, every one about the weight of a talent. A talent was the largest unit of money of the time, designed to be all that a person could comfortably transport. The weight was somewhere between 70 and 120 pounds. This knowledge gives added meaning to the parable of the talents, realizing that the servants were not entrusted with pocket change, but rather, a virtual fortune.

17
Satan's Power Broker Exposed

Chapter 17 is probably the most important chapter in understanding Satan's last-days work. John has described a number of different views of what takes place in the last days. One of the seven angels now steps forward to explain. John's previous teachings have all been in preparation for what is about to happen. He is ready to expose Satan's last-days, great and abominable secret combination.

The Great Whore

In verse 1, the image is of a fallen woman, one who will do anything for money. The outward appearance of the whore may be enticing and appealing, but inside, she is full of corruption, scheming, filthiness and abomination. The whore is upon many waters, which verse 15 translates as peoples, multitudes, nations and tongues. Only something of worldwide proportions will meet the criteria.

Verse 2 states that the kings of the earth have committed fornication with her. They have traded the souls of their nations for an ugly and evil counterfeit of something beautiful and precious. The price for this sin is paid by the inhabitants of the earth, who have been forced to drink with the wine of her fornication. Since the kings of the earth and a whore have come together, one can expect to see money included in the transaction. Satan teaches that he can buy anything in this world with money. How would he extort this money and gain this control?

The author believes he knows the answer. Just before Christmas, and very late at night in December of 1913, a time when most of the family men had gone home, the Federal Reserve Act was passed by Congress. By this act, consitutional law was put aside. Article I, Section 10 of the United States Constitution states that no state shall make anything but gold and silver coin as tender in payment of debt. Real value was replaced with something false, with this philosophy: "As long as the people think they are getting their money's worth, we can profit from this deception." Here is a simplified synopsis:

a very small group of private United States and world bankers obtained a federal charter to create a private corporation known as the Federal Reserve. This is a misnomer, for it is not federal and it has no reserves. The United States Government would print paper and call it "federal reserve accounting unit dollars." (This makes for a most interesting acronym: F.R.A.U.D.) The good name and credit of the United States would be used as backing. The United States would be reimbursed for the cost of printing and paper, then borrow these units from the Federal Reserve to put them into circulation. The taxpayers would pay back the loan, plus interest.

The Fruits of the Federal Reserve

To collect on this debt, an income tax was also established shortly thereafter. This act also violated the original Constitution (Article 1, Section 9). The inspired precepts of the Constitution were replaced with the doctrine of Karl Marx. It was a dirty, evil, secret deal. The term *fornication* is a fitting description. Through this illegitimate alliance, the whore does the earthly bidding of her master. The dependence on her money now enslaves nations, states and individuals.

Several elected officials of this time period left their impressions of the Federal Reserve Act. Congressman Charles Lindbergh, Sr. (father of the aviator) warned congress:

> This act establishes the most gigantic trust on earth. . . . When the President signs this act the invisible government by the money power, proven to exist by the Money Trust investigation, will be legalized. . . .
>
> The money power overawes the legislative and executive forces of the Nation and of the States. I have seen these forces exerted during the different stages of this bill. . . .
> (*Congressional Record,* Vol. 51, pp. 1446-47)

The chairman of the House Committee on Banking and Currency from 1920 to 1931, Congressman Louis McFadden, later stated:

> When the Federal Reserve Act was passed, the people of these United States did not perceive that a world banking system was being set up here.
>
> A superstate controlled by international bankers and international industrialists acting together to enslave the world for their own pleasure.

> Every effort has been made by the Fed to conceal its powers but the truth is—the Fed has usurped the government.
>
> (*The Unseen Hand*, p. 182)

The Federal Reserve was established by the secret combining of wealth, power, influence, and intrigue. Excellent documentation and explanation of these interests at work is found in the book, *The Creature from Jekyll Island, A Second Look at the Federal Reserve,* by G. Edward Griffin.

The stated purpose of Mr. Griffin's book is to accurately demonstrate his assertions that the Federal Reserve must be abolished because:

- It is incapable of accomplishing its stated objectives
- It is a cartel operating against the public interests
- It is the supreme instrument of usury
- It generates our most unfair tax
- It encourages war
- It destabilizes the economy
- It is an instrument of totalitarianism

Imagine a game of Monopoly (appropriately named). The tested and proven rules of fair play are manipulated and changed (the government is influenced). Instead of the bank being impartial, it is actually controlled by some of the players who not only have their existing money, but have additional money they have secretly obtained from several other games. Imagine playing the game in such a way that instead of mercifully ending, it goes on for scores of years. The controllers seek to keep all in the game paying as much (rent, usury and taxes) as they possibly can obtain. Sounds fun, doesn't it?

The marriage between monopolistic central banking and government is unauthorized by the constitution. It was written against, extensively, by Thomas Jefferson and many of the founding fathers. The disastrous results of the first national bank and the prosperity that followed its abolition and the nation's return to sound currency had taught the founding fathers a valuable lesson. Andrew Jackson was elected on a platform which included abolishing the second national bank. He called a delegation of national bank supporters a "den of vipers" and stated, "I intend to rout you out, and by the Eternal God I will rout you out." With the wealth no longer being drained off to the bankers, the Jackson Administration actually refunded money to the states at a time when there was no personal income tax. The Federal Reserve is this nation's third and potentially most disastrous flirtation with big central banking, which empowers big centralized government.

Mr. Griffin shows how much of the funding, through the Federal Reserve, of the International Monetary Fund (the I.M.F. is a world federal reserve, but is mostly backed by the U.S.) and foreign aid is used by governments to buy industries, consolidate power, and purchase armaments (a formula for socialism, tyranny, and war). Americans would never tolerate being directly taxed for such un-American activity. It is only through the hidden taxation by inflation, caused by the creation of money at the Federal Reserve, that this dubious mission is accomplished.

With this background, one can now see the whore in action. Verse 3 states that she is sitting upon a beast. The logical assumption is that the beast belongs to her. She owns it, feeds it, trains it, and is responsible for it. Later, it will be shown that this is a dangerous beast to keep, but now she seems to have it under full control. What is this beast? It is scarlet colored—the very same beast described earlier in Revelation 13:2. It is full of names of blasphemy, having seven heads and ten horns.

Today's Wine of Fornication

The red beast has already been clearly identified by the author as the Communists. John here reveals that there is a big, evil, secret entity behind, and supporting, the Communist movement. The whore is arrayed and decked with the wealth of the earth. Obviously, she has been extremely successful at her trade. Her hand is full of something that represents abominations and the filthiness of her fornication. The author believes that what she has in her hand is printed money, and lots of it. With this money, she wields great power over all the earth.

At first glance, the comparison between currency and the wine of the whore's fornication may seem to be a far stretch of the imagination. When the actual results of the two are compared, however, the analogy appears to be an excellent match. In fact, the use of the wine image reveals much additional meaning. Certainly, banknotes would have been a meaningless symbol hundreds of years before the invention of the printing press. Gold, likewise, would not accurately portray the actuality of today's economics. The fact that the wine is held in a golden cup (has the appearance of holding great value) by a woman arrayed with the world's wealth (Revelation 17:4), and how she is using this wine (Revelation 17:6), certainly matches currency much more accurately than any wine the author is familiar with. In effect, both wine and money can be very addictive opiates, suppressors of consciousness, and seem to incline people to abandon their morality.

In witnessing this nation's slip from its constitutional republic roots toward the socialistic welfare state, one can see great quantities of money used to put, and keep, the public asleep. Also present are all kinds of soul-destroying addictions. Like cheap wine, some are addicted to social programs that destroy independence, initiative, and eventually, the soul. Others are addicted to expensively packaged, but equally deadly, power, position, dominion, and unfair advantage—ultimately sacrificing their independence, initiative, and soul for their next financial fix. Like the addicted alcoholic, few admit to the disease. They believe they can stop any time they really want. Eventually, however, it must be recognized that all addiction is bondage. This is especially evident in the behavior of state and local governments as they clamor for more and more federal funds.

The prophet Isaiah may have been using the same imagery as found in Revelation. He refers to a time after the faithful city became a harlot, when "Thy silver is become dross, thy wine mixed with water" (Isaiah 1:22). Inflation certainly has this effect. Not only is paper currency devalued as additional money is created, but the silver in U.S. coinage has been replaced with dross. Dross literally means the base metals left over after the refining of gold and silver. Inflation is often referred to as a tax, but few ever bother to find out the simple explanation as to the who, what, why, where, when, and how this tax is actually collected and used.

There have been many good books written exposing the Federal Reserve for what it is, a government-protected central bank monopoly, providing vast wealth for its controllers, and creating the ability for government to borrow and use unlimited funds at the expense of the American people, but without their direct consent, knowledge, or approval. The author again recommends the book, *The Creature from Jekyll Island,* to demystify this process. Isaiah further states that in the last days, the people would wonder, cry out, and be drunken, but not with wine, and stagger, but not with strong drink, followed by a condition of a deep sleep (Isaiah 29:9,10). Interestingly, the antidote prescribed in this chapter of Isaiah for the condition is the coming forth of the sealed book (*The Book of Mormon*). *The Book of Mormon* contains the greatest expose' of secret combinations available today. So that the reader does not become complacent thinking that this is just a problem in the "world," Isaiah devotes an entire chapter as a woe unto the drunkards in Ephraim (Isaiah 28).

The Woman's Thirst for Blood

Upon the woman's head a name is written—"Mystery," for her workings are in the dark and her ways are not widely known—followed by the name "Babylon the Great." In days gone by, Babylon ruled the known world. Her influence was everywhere. A latter-day equivalent can now be seen. The next title is "Mother of Harlots." She multiplies and spreads her evil work. The final description is "Abominations of the Earth." John is impressed by the magnitude of what she is doing. It is felt in all the earth.

Here is something big, evil, secret and multiplying. This woman is the great enemy to God. She is drunk with the blood of the saints, and with the blood of the martyrs of Jesus. She kills on a grand scale those who oppose her. The whore is doing what she is doing for the love of money, her fornication with kings has to do with debt and usury, and the whore is Satanic and evil. Could she be increasing her trade by promoting the greatest national debt creation tool ever devised, even war? Such a scenario would account for her blood-drinking binges. Those who died in opposition to the work of the whore Babylon were referred to as saints and martyrs of Jesus. The prophet Mormon seems to be describing this same situation:

> Behold, I speak unto you as if ye were present, and yet ye are not. But behold, Jesus Christ hath shown you unto me, and I know your doing.
>
> And I know that ye do walk in the pride of your hearts; and there are none save a few only who do not lift themselves up in the pride of their hearts, unto the wearing of very fine apparel, unto envying, and strifes, and malice, and persecutions, and all manner of iniquities; and your churches, yea, even every one, have become polluted because of the pride of your hearts.
>
> Yea, why do ye build up your secret abominations to get gain, and cause that widows should mourn before the Lord, and also orphans to mourn before the Lord, and also the blood of their fathers and their husbands to cry unto the Lord from the ground, for vengeance upon your heads?
>
> Behold, the sword of vengeance hangeth over you; and the time soon cometh that he avengeth the blood of the saints upon you, for he will not suffer their cries any longer.
>
> (Mormon 8:35-36; 40-41)

What is it that has so specifically robbed this nation of the blood of its husbands and fathers? The author believes it could only be war. Mormon, like John, also honors the sacrifice and righteous intents of those who gave their all in freedom's cause. The blood spilt in this cause is the blood of Saints. No one should forget what the fields of white crosses represent.

Scripturally, secret combinations are always associated with bloodshed and war. This last-days pattern follows what occurred among Nephites in ancient America. The culprit is pride. Pride creates enmity to God through a lust for riches, power, pleasure, and sin, above all else. In this condition, secret combinations are spawned and flourish. Proverbs teaches that only by pride cometh contention, and pride goeth before destruction (Proverbs 13:10, 16-18).

In verse 7, the angel tells John that he will explain the mystery of the woman and her beast. Twice in verse 8 he states that the beast "was, and is not, and yet is." If the beast is the former communist Soviet Union, then it is important to remember that this is a nation that "was," but "is not," yet it shall rise out of the bottomless pit to do its work before it goes into perdition.

John is told that the people of the earth wonder, except for a few who know what is going on, whose names are written in the book of life. How is it that some of the elect seem to know what to expect? Should people seek to recognize and expose this great worldwide secret combination of abominations? For the Latter-day Saints, the Lord gives this admonition:

> Therefore, that we should waste and wear out our lives in bringing to light all the hidden things of darkness, wherein we know them; and they are truly manifest from heaven—
> These should then be attended to with great earnestness.
> Let no man count them as small things; for there is much which lieth in futurity, pertaining to the saints, which depends upon these things.
> You know, brethren, that a very large ship is benefited very much by a very small helm in the time of a storm, by being kept workways with the wind and the waves.
> Therefore, dearly beloved brethren, let us cheerfully do all things that lie in our power; and then may we stand still, with the utmost assurance, to see the salvation of God, and for his arm to be revealed.
> (D & C 123:13-17)

The Unpopular Conspiracy Theories

It is presently very vogue to discount the conspiracy theory. It is popular to point fingers, laugh and scorn those who hold onto such simple beliefs as a continuation of the war in heaven on this earth, a war that was fought over the free agency of God's children. Those who try to bring to light the secret works of darkness are looked upon as fanatical, paranoid, or mentally unbalanced. Conspiracies are not talked about on the news, taught in schools, or expanded on by any but a few national leaders. On the other hand, the latter-day seeker of truth must shake his head in amazement that so many refuse to see something so big and so obvious. It is like someone denying the existence of an elephant in his living room just because it isn't supposed to be there.

The scriptures demonstrate which side of the pointing fingers it is safest to be on. Historically, it seems that most of the people have been wrong most of the time. The writings of the prophet Enoch show that secret works of darkness have before deceived the *whole* earth, and Christ said this day would be as the days of Noah. It is essential to know and love the Book of Mormon, a book which testifies that the destruction of two great nations came about because of massive, evil, secret combinations that subverted governments, deceived and manipulated the people, caused warfare and strife, and bore a striking resemblances to what can be seen in the world today. The Book of Mormon speaks from the dust to warn of similar secret combinations that are present today (Ether 8:18-26; Alma 37:25-32).

It is also important to know and love the living prophets and the words of truth they teach. Know that the Lord raises prophets up, giving them life experiences and schooling to be the Lord's mouthpiece for a given time. Their calling is not an accident; the prophet's life and learning are part of his message. The life teachings and understanding presented by President Ezra Taft Benson, in his many talks and books, may prove to be a great key to understanding and overcoming the hidden things of darkness today. Elder Ezra Taft Benson once stated, in the Converence Report dated October 1961, p. 74 said, "We should accept the command of the Lord and treat socialistic communism as the tool of Satan. We should follow the counsel of the President of the Church and resist the influence and policies of the socialist-communist conspiracy wherever they are found—in the schools, in the churches, in governments, in unions, in businesses, in agriculture." This indicated that he was aware of the conspiracy's infiltration into all of these arenas. The name

Ezra Taft Benson, former Secretary of Agriculture, appears as an endorsement upon the cover of a book called None Dare Call It Conspiracy, by Gary Allen. This book exposes a secret combination that exactly fits within the framework of the description given by John for the whore Babylon. Apostle Benson writes, "I wish that every citizen of every country in the free world, and every slave behind the iron curtain, might read this book."

Some might say he was only an apostle when he held such strong views; they may have missed President Benson's October 1988 conference talk titled "I Testify," or not noticed that the book *Teachings of Ezra Taft Benson* was published after he became church President, and with the blessings and approval of the First Presidency. Others believe it is because of these strong, albeit unpopular beliefs, that he was chosen to be the mouthpiece of God at the critical time of the church's and nation's history that he served.

For many, the search for truth began with the book *The Naked Communist*, written by a patient and studious observer, W. Cleon Skousen. It was President David O. McKay who encouraged Brother Skousen to personally publish this book after it was rejected by the major publishers. This great work was, for many, the first good look at the red beast. On page 347 of President Benson's tremendous book, *God, Family, Country,* the apostle states, "During the general conference of the Church, in October 1959, President David O. McKay, in discussing the threat of communism, referred to W. Cleon Skousen's book *The Naked Communist* and said, 'I admonish everybody to read that excellent book.' He then quoted the following from the flyleaf: 'The conflict between communism and freedom is the problem of our time. It overshadows all other problems.'" How many have followed that admonition of the prophet?

Skousen's book is still a great primer for anyone seeking to know of this scarlet beast called communism. After W. Cleon Skousen's later book, *The Naked Capitalist*, the world in general received extensive knowledge of how this secret entity, (equated, here, with the whore Babylon), actually financed and sponsored the communistic/socialistic movement here and abroad. *The Naked Capitalist* is a synopsis of an extensive work by Professor Carroll Quigley. Professor Quigley's name may be familiar to some, since Bill Clinton, during his acceptance speech as the Democratic Party's candidate for President of the United States, named two figures who had influenced his philosophies and inspired him in his desires for public office. John F. Kennedy was the first, and his former college professor, Carroll Quigley, was the other. Dr. Quigley belonged to the inner circles of a group of super-rich, super-powerful, and super-secret exploiters. He lauded their philosophies and goals, but disagreed with their insistence on carefully-guarded secrecy. Following is a quote from Dr. Quigley's book:

> The aim of the international bankers is "nothing less than to create a world system of financial control in private hands able to dominate the political system of each country, and the economy of the world as a whole. The system will be controlled in a feudal fashion, by the central banks of the world acting in concert, by SECRET agreements arrived at in frequent PRIVATE meetings and conferences." [Such as Bilderbergers.]
>
> The individual's "freedom and choice WILL BE CONTROLLED within very NARROW alternatives by the fact that he will be numbered from birth and followed, as a number, through his educational training, his required military or other public service, his tax contributions, his health and medical requirements, and his final retirement and death benefits."
>
> (*Tragedy and Hope, A History of the World in Our Time*, p. 324)

The admonition of the brethren to study this inspired Constitution and the books previously mentioned, begins a journey of discovery into the virtual explosion of research, books, and publications currently available. This prescribed study, combined with scriptural research, provides the tools to separate truth from error. To emphasize the importance of not being "asleep" as the means of avoiding captivity, the words of Father Lehi cry from the dust:

> O that ye would awake; awake from a deep sleep, yea, even from the sleep of hell, and shake off the awful chains by which ye are bound, which are the chains which bind the children of men, that they are carried away captive down to the eternal gulf of misery and woe.
>
> (2 Nephi 1:13)

There is no conspiracy theory within the pages of John's Revelation, the Pearl of Great Price, Doctrine & Covenants, and the Book of Mormon. There is only, as President Benson said, conspiracy fact. The scriptures are replete with evidence and warnings of a huge, highly organized, worldwide Satanic conspiracy of evil in this day. The author encourages the reader to inform himself of these secret combinations, carefully studying the scriptures and considering the evidences in this book.

The Whore and Beast Grow in Power

In returning to verses 9-11, it is seen that the whore has a long history. It seems that secret combinations are Satan's method of operation. The seven heads of the beast are the seven Satanic churches built on earth to Satan's specification. Just as Christ establishes his church on earth seven distinct times, Satan has set up his counterfeit. It is easier to see Satan's hand clearly and distinctly in dispensations gone by, but harder to look and see his work in the present day. This near-sightedness is a Satanic trick. Just as Christ offers the spiritual and political kingdom in righteousness, the great and abominable church in each dispensation is a combined political and spiritual kingdom controlled by Satan.

So that it cannot be overlooked, once again verse 11 points out that the beast in the last days was, and is not, and yet goes into perdition. John does not want anyone to miss this very important characteristic of the red beast. Those who wish to sleepily follow the current trend of media hype into believing that communism is prematurely finished may be caught unprepared. John repeats this important fact five times. He must be giving it special attention for a good reason. The scarlet beast (Communist Russia) is not dead (Revelation 13:3, 13:12, 13:14, 17:8, 17:11).

Verse 12 teaches of ten would-be kings seeking kingdoms. They receive power as kings one hour with the beast. This single-minded combination gives strength and power to the beast (verse 13). These ten kings are represented as ten horns upon the beast. This is an evil, short-lived, but powerful combination, and possibly the reason the head of the beast is miraculously restored. It is at this point that the forces of Satan make war with the forces of the Lamb. This is one time when reading the scriptures will pay big dividends. This battle is rigged, the outcome decided. Standing victorious on the side of the Lamb "are they that are with him, called, chosen, and faithful" (Revelation 17:14). The prophet Daniel also describes the last-day worldly kingdom being crushed by a kingdom set up by Christ. This is represented by a stone cut out of the mountain without hands and rolling forth. The last-days worldly kingdom is represented as the feet of the image with ten toes (Daniel 2:32, 33, 41, 44). Cross-reference the ten toes of the image with the ten horns on this beast.

Verse 16 shows that the beast, which the whore is keeping, is a most dangerous beast to keep. It seems the beast does not like being controlled, manipulated, sat on and used. It will hate the whore. The destruction of the whore Babylon will come because the beast will take her wealth, remove the covering of her nakedness, devour her people, and burn her with fire. Being a member of Babylon's great and spacious building or club does not give assurance of security.

Verse 17 states what has been stated many times before in scripture—that it is by the wicked that the wicked are destroyed. So that the identity of the whore is perfectly clear, the woman is described in verse 18. It is the great city. Anciently Babylon was a city, a people, and a world influence. The word great is used so that the reader will look for something of colossal proportions. The power and influence of the whore "reign over the kings of the earth." If one looks for anything less than a power so great that it rules and controls the leaders of nations, he will miss seeing the mystery of Babylon the great. The workings of the dragon, or Satan, are now mapped out. He is working through a beast, the image of the beast, and a second beast. This is all coordinated by the whore Babylon, who has great wealth, works in secret, commits fornication or has immoral alliances with the kings of the earth, and forces the inhabitants of the earth to drink with the wine of the wrath of her fornication. Temporal and spiritual salvation may depend on being able to see.

18
Babylon is Destroyed

Following the description of the whore Babylon, chapter 18 of Revelation is a call for the righteous to come out of her and not be partakers of her destruction and plagues. Babylon, great though she be, will fall. The God of heaven has decreed it.

Verse 3 again states that all nations have drunk of the wine of the wrath of her fornication. One also sees that the merchants of the earth have waxed rich through the abundance of her delicacies. Anciently, Babylon, represented by the golden head of the image in the dream Daniel interpreted, was the richest of all kingdoms that would follow it for over two thousand years. Modern Babylon shares this abundant wealth. The destroyers of Babylon are instructed to show her no mercy, and reward her double, according to her works. She is to see sorrow and torment in proportion to her self-glorification and delicious living by her ill-gotten gains. Her wealth and riches have been accumulated at the expense of others' lives and freedoms. This is another indication that her fornication could be tied to usury and plunder.

The last sentence in verse 7 is a reflection on the attitudes of the leaders and people of the earth. The fornicating whore sits exalted as a queen and wife. The flatterers, courtly socialites, favor-seekers and subjects, all act as if this is a normal relationship, even though many must surely recognize that this is an abominable disgrace.

The Destruction of Ancient Babylon

The destruction of modern Babylon will bring death, mourning, famine and a fire so intense that she will utterly be burned. Her destruction comes in one day, or one hour of one day. The one-hour figure is mentioned twice in this chapter. It is reminiscent of the destruction of ancient Babylon in the days of Daniel the prophet. Belshazzar, son of King Nebuchachnezzer, became king and called a huge feast. The guests included one thousand of his lords. In mockery and blasphemy, the vessels of the temple were used in a drunken orgy. The finger of God wrote upon the wall, and Daniel was called in to interpret.

First of all, Daniel listed the sins of King Belshazzar:
1. he humbled not himself.
2. he sinned with a full knowledge.
3. he lifted up himself against the Lord of heaven.
4. he praised gods of silver, gold, brass, iron, wood and stone.
5. he glorified not God.

The writing on the wall was interpreted as "God hath numbered thy kingdom and finished it. Thou art weighed in the balances and found wanting. The kingdom shall be divided and given to the Medes and Persians."

The city of Babylon was considered by the experts of the day to be impregnable. Its very high city walls were wide enough for a road and houses on the top. Yet the city fell that very night. Darius, the Median, simply diverted the river and marched his troops under the wall (see Daniel 5).

The Destruction of Present Babylon

There are probably many similarities between modern and ancient Babylon. Just as ancient Babylon was represented as both a city and a worldwide influence, the destruction of modern Babylon seems to also indicate a place, or places, and a specific act of destruction. Kings of the earth are seen standing afar off, for fear of her torment. The fact that they are in fear of the torment of her burning and are not rushing to her aid would certainly seem to suggest a nuclear destruction. This place is a world marketplace, and a major port. Everything and anything is for sale here, including the souls of men. This port city is so important that every shipmaster and sailor, again standing afar off, will mourn her loss. They say, "What city is like unto this city?"

Amidst all the bewailing is heard a call from heaven for the holy apostles and prophets to rejoice over her destruction. The wickedness of this great city has been aimed against them, so God hath avenged them on her. It will be remembered that the destruction of ancient Babylon actually improved the lot of Daniel (he was made first of the presidents) and his close associates, Shadrach, Meshach, and Abed-nego. It may be assumed that this was an improvement for the whole of captive Israel. The destruction of ancient Babylon came at a gathering of the princes of Babylon, so they were all destroyed. The fall of ancient Babylon cleared the way for the return and rebuilding of Jerusalem. It was to this rebuilt Jerusalem that Christ came in the flesh. This is similar to, or a type of, the destruction that will occur before New Jerusalem is built.

Verse 21 depicts a mighty angel who takes a great millstone and casts it into the sea, saying, "Thus with violence shall that great city Babylon be thrown down, and shall be found no more at all." This is reminiscent of Christ's saying in the New Testament that for anyone who harms one of his little ones, it would be better for them that a millstone were hung around their neck, and they were drowned in the depths of the sea. Babylon the great, the cause of so much suffering among the innocent, shall rise no more.

One can learn more of the workings of this great city in reading what is "found no more" in association with her. This city will no longer be a center for music; no longer a place where all crafts are practiced; no longer a great, noisy industrial center; no longer a place where the light of its candle will shine; no longer a place for weddings and merriment; and no longer the place where the greatest merchants of the earth gather. From this city went forth the sorcery that deceived all nations. Underneath it is blood—the blood of righteous prophets and saints.

The last line of verse 24 is very important: "and of all that were slain upon the earth." The scripture states that upon this city, people and worldwide influence is an element of responsibility for all the killing that has occurred in the last days. Only a truly Luciferian combination could have such an all-encompassing influence. All of the murder over money, power, and greed; all of the martyrs over religion and freedom; and all of the ideologic conflicts are somehow tied to the work being done in secret from this one great and wicked city.

19
Preparation for the Marriage Supper

With the destruction of the great whore Babylon, its secret institutions and worldly influence removed, it is now possible to prepare for the marriage supper of the Lamb. The first verses of chapter 19 were filled with "Alleluias." For the righteous invited to the supper to meet our Lord, the most "dreadful" part is over and the "great" experiences remain to be fulfilled.

So that there is no mistake about the judgments of God upon the whore Babylon, verse 2 again states that his judgments are "true and righteous" against the whore. She corrupted the earth with her fornication. This is repeated often, so it must be very important to know what her fornication is. Stated again is the belief that it is the illegitimate alliances created by trading money for control among the kings of the earth. Only this combination of money, wealth, and power could bear a degree of responsibility for the slaying of all righteous. For this, Cain slew his brother Abel, and so it has been with the wicked ever after. The author believes that the true motivation for murder and genocide has been, and always will be, the robbery and control of their property. This Satanic killing to get gain is the secret that unifies the most wicked, from Cain, to Gadianton, to Lenin, to those doing the killing today. God's people know and understand that without property rights, the pursuit of life, liberty, and happiness is impossible. Satan's followers have always been willing to kill to rob and steal and control that which belongs to another.

God has now avenged the blood of his servants. The angels rejoice as the smoke of Babylon goes up forever and ever. Alleluia, Amen.

The bride—the woman, or church—struggling to bring forth the kingdom of God on earth as it is in heaven, has now made herself ready. She is cleansed and dressed in fine white linen, which is the righteousness of the saints. It is no small thing to be unified with the king of heaven and earth. The preparation, purifying, and cleansing have been difficult; but those called to the supper can now see that it was necessary to prepare them to be worthy to be present at the wedding.

To the supper, the long-awaited bridegroom arrives. The Lamb, the great king, the Lord God omnipotent, is united with his people. In jealousy and rage, Satan blasphemously cries, "I should be at the supper." He gathers his hosts of uninvited guests--the beast, the kings of the earth, and their armies—together. The woman, weak and drained by her preparation, surely would not be able to stand alone; but now married (united with Christ) to her husband, she is safe and protected.

An eleven-year-old Latter-day Saint girl related the following experience in her journal:

> I had a really good dream last night, and here it is.
>
> It was at a wedding reception. Everything was going okay; then a stranger walked in. His clothes were new, but yet, clothes that would be worn in another country a long time ago. He sat and listened. He wasn't invited to the wedding, but was allowed to stay at once. Then refreshments came. He sat by me. I ate my food; he ate not. He handed me a piece of his bread; I ate it. It tasted like manna. I looked at him closely. I knew him. He was Jesus. He then blessed everyone; then I woke up. I felt really good inside.

Her dream contained symbolism of the marriage of the Lamb, the bread of life, and his sudden coming. Children are sometimes the greatest teachers.

The heavens are opened. Christ, who rode into Jerusalem on a colt, is now seen sitting upon his white horse under the banner of the king. An earthly army of 200 million is simply no match for the divine king. The final battle is short-lived, for the beast with his false prophet, and the believers in his promised miracles (to bring forth a righteous kingdom on earth without the righteous king would indeed be miraculous), along with those still wearing the mark of the beast, or who are worshipping his image, are cast alive into the lake of fire and brimstone (Revelation 19:20).

20
Satan Banished as the Millennium Begins

With the destruction of the wicked on earth complete, Satan himself must be banished. For six thousand years, he has ruled from a place described simply as a bottomless pit. The term *bottomless* refers to the fact that all things truly have their opposites—eternal progression and glory by following Christ, or eternal digression and hell by following his enemy. After six thousand years of rule and great power, Satan must have felt the owner of this world. However, from Revelation 21:1 it is learned that he doesn't even own the key to his own house. An angel from heaven locks and closes the door behind him.

Moses 7:26 teaches that during Enoch and Noah's time, Satan had a great chain in his hand, and with it he veiled the whole face of the earth with darkness. Likewise, in these last days, Satan again has been using his great chain to powerfully lead and bind the minds of men. John reiterates in this chapter that the way Satan perpetrated his greatest evil was to "deceive the nations." Later, when Satan is loosed from the thousand-year period of being bound, he will loosed once again to "deceive the nations." An angel from heaven has taken the chain of darkness away, and metaphorically used it to seal the prison house wherein Satan is bound. This chain, created personally with so much work, care, and Satanic delight, stands between Satan and the joy of the saints for one thousand years.

Verse 4 shows a group of people who are not only living with Christ, but reigning with him for the one thousand years. As John describes them, he may be teaching something about the order of the Satanic challenges to the saints of the last days. He first mentions those that were beheaded for the witness of Jesus. Remembering that John is trying to reveal, not hide, truth, one can recognize that in the present day, beheading is associated with the Satanic bloodbath of the socialistic French Revolution. The Christian, the free man, the good and honorable, along with those whose property was coveted, were, and ever since have been, targets of the socialistic/communistic revolutionaries. As learned from President Benson, "When a man stands for freedom, he stands for God; and as long as he stands for freedom, he stands with God. And were he to stand alone, he would still stand with God" (*An Enemy Hath Done This,* p. 55). The promise is fulfilled in that these martyrs are standing with God. This is followed by the judgement of those who had not worshipped the beast, neither his image, and had not received his mark in their foreheads or in their hands.

The rest of the dead, those who followed Satan, do not live again for one thousand years. The author believes that it is more than just a coincidence that with the resurrection of those who were deceived by Satan while living on earth, the release of Satan from his prison house follows. Unrepentant, and numbered as the sands of the sea, these once again go to make war led by Satan, and joined by Gog and Magog. From D & C 88:111-113 it is learned that when Satan is loosed for this little season to gather his armies, Michael, the archangel, will be gathering together his armies, including the hosts of heaven. While the hosts of hell compass about the saints and the beloved city, they are once again devoured—this time by fire from heaven. The devil that deceived them is cast into the lake of fire and brimstone, where the beast and the false prophets are. Forever and ever they are tormented, day and night. With each other for company, there is probably little need for additional divine torment.

The dead, small and great, must face God. At this judgment bar are many books. The records have been kept faithfully, but one in particular stands out: The book of life—perhaps more specifically, the book of your life, written with the pen of your footprints in daily living. Judgment is according to works; those not found written in the book of life are overcome by the second death. Those who have still chosen darkness over light are now shut out spiritually from the great light of the universe, the kingdom of our Christ, and of his God, forever and ever.

21
The Righteous Enter Christ's Presence

Revelation 20 views the millennium from the viewpoint of the wicked. Chapters 21 and 22 contain the view as seen by those who are worthy to be there with Christ. The Book of Revelation is an invitation sent out with plenty of advance notice so that all can be there. All will need to work on their vesture, the white linen which is the righteousness of the saints. They will also need sufficient oil to overcome the darkness of night before the arrival of the Glorious Son. Those whose lights have gone out will be shut outside the gates of glory.

With Christ comes newness, regeneration, and resurrection. The earth and the heavens are renewed. Even the memory of the telestial earth is fading far away. Just as with resurrected beings, who are now flesh and bone (no mention of blood), so the earth itself no longer has a sea (Revelation 21:1). Returning to earth as a bride adorned for her husband are the churches of Enoch's and Melchizedek's days. The temple, or tabernacle of heaven, is returned from the clouds, and God himself is with them. The covenants of Enoch and Noah are fulfilled:

> And a bow shall be in the cloud; and I will look upon it, that I may remember the everlasting covenant, which I made unto thy father Enoch; that, when men should keep all my commandments, Zion should again come on earth, the city of Enoch which I have caught up unto myself.
>
> And this is mine everlasting covenant, that when thy posterity shall embrace the truth, and look upward, then shall Zion look downward, and all the heavens shall shake with gladness, and the earth shall tremble with joy;
>
> And the general assembly of the church of the first-born shall come down out of heaven, and possess the earth, and shall have place until the end come. And this is mine everlasting covenant, which I made with thy father Enoch.
>
> (Joseph Smith Translation, Genesis 9:21-23)

It is especially enlightening to read the language John uses to describe his going to the great city, Holy Jerusalem, that descends out of heaven from God. He describes it as being carried away in the spirit to a great and high mountain (Revelation 21:10). Others have used this same language of the prophets to describe their experiences.

As the telestial earth passes away, so do pain, crying, sorrow, death, and the tears which Christ shall personally wipe away from the eyes of the righteous. Those who have given their all for Christ now receive their inheritance. The gift of grace and love includes everything, all that the Father hath, including a restoration of the eternal relationship with Christ. How silly it will then seem to have tried to hold anything back, to have tried to keep some of this telestial hell in exchange for eternal glory!

As a reminder of what must be left behind, those characteristics which are not compatible to bring into the exalted presence of God are listed for the last time beginning with verse 8. Topping the list is fear—fear that keeps one from acting, doing and living as he knows he should. Since the Lord judges people by what they do, it is critical to overcome fearfulness. Only when one moves his feet can God direct his steps. People who never do anything do not make mistakes, except the biggest mistake of all.

Second on the list is to be unbelieving. The skeptic, the cynic, and those with unfertile soil for faith will have their part in the second death. The filthy, corrupt abomination-seekers are likewise cast out. Those who would kill and destroy to get gain will be with their father, who was a murderer from the beginning. Those who would use and hold another in a sinful condition have no part with Christ. It is interesting that the curse is directed at the abusive controller, or the whoremonger, rather than the whore. The sorcerer, the seeker of power, will find that it was all an illusion, a grand lie. Those who worshipped that which was created rather than the Creator—the idolater—along with lying deceivers, complete the list.

One can almost feel the enthusiasm as one of the seven angels approaches John, saying, "Come hither, and I will show thee the bride, the Lamb's wife, even the great city, holy Jerusalem, descending out of heaven from God."

For four thousand years, Enoch and his people have been building. The city has been raised by a people who, through priesthood ordination, keys and faith, have power over even the elements.

> For God having sworn unto Enoch and unto his seed with an oath by himself; that everyone being ordained after this order and calling

shall have power, by faith, to break mountains, to divide the seas, to dry up waters, to turn them out of their course.
(Joseph Smith Translation, Genesis 14:30)

The workmanship of this temple/city is exquisite. Most impressive is the city's size. If present translation and interpretation is correct, the city is over 1300 miles wide, 1300 miles long, and 1300 miles high. The cubic shape of the city is symbolic of perfection and fullness, and is reminiscent of the shape of the Holy of Holies. The shape also reminds one of the personal need to be squared away in the solid principles of perfection. The city has twelve stories, one on top of each other, and twelve gates, three on each side. The workmanship is such that there is no need for a temple within, for the entire city itself is a temple. The burning of Christ's glory lights the city day and night, without any need for any other source of light. Citizenship in this great city is a gift to all those whose names are written in the Lamb's book of life.

22
The Holy City

Upon entering the last chapter of the Revelation, one can see a pure river: the river of the water of life, proceeding out of the throne of God and the Lamb. On either side of the river, so as to be readily accessible, is the tree of life. The tree yields twelve manners of fruits monthly. These provide powerful medicine for the healing of the nations and the removal of the curse. The servants who will serve Christ will see and be familiar with the face of their master. All of this must shortly be done: "Behold, I come quickly."

John is overcome with the glory and light of what he has seen: the angel, the city, the waters, the tree of life, and the throne where God sits. He falls down to worship at the feet of the angel, but is quickly rebuked. The angel is one of his exalted and glorified brothers in the gospel, one of the prophets, like himself.

John is told that this portion of the revelation is not to be sealed. He states once again that Christ is come to restore, not to remake. Wickedness will be restored to wickedness, and righteousness to righteousness (Alma 41:10). With Christ comes his reward:

> And, behold, I come quickly; and my reward is with me, to give every man according as his work shall be.
>
> (Revelation 22:12)

Jesus Christ sent his angel so that the world would have this testimony and revelation. The invitation of the book is summarized and repeated in Revelation 22:17:

> And the Spirit and the bride say, "Come. And let him that heareth say, Come. And let him that is athirst come. And whosoever will, let him take the water of life freely."

The book ends with a final warning to the wicked who would change, alter, or destroy the words of this book. Much of vast importance in latter-days comes through this record. It is vitally important that the world see John's record in its original form. More is known about the nature of Satan, his secret works of darkness, and his last-day agenda from this book than the rest of the books of the Bible combined. It teaches even more about the nature, blessing and glory of Christ.

John finishes with this testimony, to which is added the author's Amen:

> He which testifieth these things saith, Surely I come quickly. Amen. Even so, come, Lord Jesus.
> The grace of our Lord Jesus Christ be with you all. Amen.
> (Revelation 22:20-21)

Conclusion

This finishes the study of John's revelation, using a context of today to unlock it's meaning. Much of the writing in Revelation has come in the form of code. In any coded message there is a sender, a receiver, and someone who may have access to the message, but not the meaning. These persons, or groups, must be understood to unlock the message. The challenge accepted by this book is to restore the meaning to John's text, using keys available to latter-day saints today. Revelation has been viewed as if it was specifically meant to be understood. The author has assumed that the keys needed to unlock this mystery are:
- the individual, church and world events of today.
- the scripture and words of prophets and leaders available today.
- the knowledge about John and his context of writing.
- the workings of the same spirit with which John's revelation was written.

If this quest has been successful, then John's writing should be "plain and pure, and most precious and easy to the understanding of all men" (1 Nephi 14:23). Neither John nor Nephi, in describing this work, said that the message would be popular, or in line with the mainstream thinking of the day, or easy to believe, or even easy to hear. In fact, John himself greatly marveled at what Satan was going to be able to accomplish in this day by his work of deception. The scriptures available in the last days teach that Satan is extremely successful in deceiving this generation. It seems that Satan's deception is much easier for most to accept over the truth and reality which can be confirmed by Christ's spirit. If it were not for this deceived state of world affairs, there may not have even been a need for John to write in a coded message. The power of John's message is that it specifically maps out what needs to be known to not only survive through the troubled times of the last days, but to be able and worthy to meet Christ as he begins his glorious millennial reign.

Look again at the power, glory, and beauty John communicates in the short 22 chapters of Revelation. John begins by telling who he is, why he is writing, how to understand his work, and pronounces a blessing upon those who will make the effort necessary to hear and understand his writing. As in any good manual providing leadership, the mission, tasks, and obstacles are clearly defined. Most importantly, at the forefront of John's writing is the goal, eternal life with Christ, and the ideals of Zion with its heavenly peace, happiness, and righteous progression.

Like the doctrines of John's master teacher, Jesus Christ, his writings first focus on the individual before he teaches the state of the world. The judgment of the churches gives tremendous insights and standards for all to examine their own lives as church members today. Christ's examples that emphasize this priority are the cleansing of the inner cup, the removal of the beam in one's own eye, and the whole of the Sermon on the Mount, where the first teachings are to perfect oneself, followed by teachings to bless others. Christ's emphasis was upon perfecting the individual as a method to improve the world.

The context of the last days is shown in relation to other periods of the earth's temporal existence with the opening of the seven seals. The events of this day are given more attention and detail. An understanding of how the works of Christ are manifest throughout the earth's history, and how all the seals fit together, is given.

John next introduces seven plagues, and the specific order in which they will occur. This information may be among the most important for temporal salvation today. Just as the children of Israel were given advance notice of the plagues in the days of Moses, so are people similarly blessed in the last days.

The events of the last days are related from several different perspectives so that the reader may more fully understand them. Events are seen from the perspective of Palestine, the Americas, the righteous, the wicked, the church, and the world, as well as from the vantage point of some of the specific groups and people of today.

With a rudimentary understanding of the *what* and *how* of events leading to those of the last days, John begins to teach *why*. He introduces the great dragon, the old serpent called the devil and Satan. A premortal war in heaven was fought. Satan, the liar from the beginning, had deceived one-third of the heavenly host into believing and fighting for his plan, whereby he promised salvation in exchange for the free agency of his followers. The war continues on this earth. This premortal war is the likeness of what is being experienced now.

In introducing the kingdoms that Satan controls in the last days, John teaches in an order—from the most obvious to an inside exposé and confirmation of that which is most mysterious. He first shows a red or scarlet beast, matching the description of the Communist's Soviet Union. From the book of Moses it is learned that God's work and glory is "to bring to pass the immortality and eternal life of man" (Moses 1:39). Satan's system is doomed from the start, producing results far short of the goal for God's children. Satan's system not only is a lie doomed to failure, but robs God's children of intended blessings. The parallel can be seen today with the failure on earth of many communistic countries.

The Book of Revelation repeatedly emphasizes (five times) that there will be a time in which this Satanic kingdom, or head of the scarlet beast, will only appear dead. This first beast is promoted by a second worldly organization that is noted for its speech, has power to kill, to call down fire from heaven in the sight of men, and tells the world that they should make an image to the first beast. This second beast matches the description of the United Nations. The prophets have taught that the worldly system which most closely resembles communism in its ultimate effect upon free agency is socialism. Socialism, then, matches this understanding of the image of the beast. This is further clarified as John teaches that the image of the beast becomes an economic system of total financial control. Those who worship the image of the beast (look to this socialistic system for their salvation) are marked as owned by it. This act of being marked is a rejection of Christ. Six times John warns of this economic system (socialism) that is the image of the beast (communism). With the exception of those carrying Christ's seal, this economic system eventually controls all of the world's commerce. Satan's system is always based upon control. John teaches that this complete economic control is the ultimate objective of the image of the beast. The challenge is to look and see Satan's influence in those earthly organizations that would lead up to this control.

So that one does not get lopsided in his views, John then shows that Christ's works are also going forth during this same period. John begins this description by showing Christ, standing upon Mt. Zion with 144,000 specially sealed servants. The gospel is restored through an angelic ministry. Christ's gospel is preached to every nation, kindred, tongue, and people. Christ's kingdom remains standing, while all of Satan's kingdom and people fall and are destroyed.

John then goes into even greater detail to reveal the great mystery he was shown through an angel. This causes John to marvel and wonder, with great admiration, at the extent of the exploits of an entity titled the *whore Babylon*. It would be a mistake to attribute the great latter-day work of Christ's kingdom to a nebulous, unorganized labor for good. It is equally unprofitable to not attribute to Satan those specific organizations described in Revelation. The challenge is that when specific acts and attributes are described, to look and identify the specific players of this day. In the Book of Mormon, the plunderers, with their government system of elitist control, were known as robbers. In the last days, the plundering whore, with her government system that rules over the kings of the earth, sits exalted as a queen and wife. She is so big that all nations have drunk of the wine of the wrath of her fornication. Of the whore Babylon, it states that she sits on, or controls, nations, kindreds, tongues, and people. She sits on and controls the scarlet beast understood to be the communists. She has great wealth and power. She is drunken with the blood of saints and the martyrs of Jesus. She uses her fornication and whoredom as an instrument of control over the kings of the earth. These kings, caught in her whoredom, may at first think they are using and controlling the whore, and getting something of value. As an unholy union it may feel good for a while, but it is empty, hollow, very costly, and leads to the destruction of those people involved. An earthly system of economic control, based upon debt, usury, and non-backed, printed paper money, matches this description today.

The scarlet beast (the Soviet Union) that was, and is not, gains a new head from its previous head and is joined in a like-minded confederacy with ten kings. These give to this beast their kingdoms. From here, the beast destroys by fire its master, the whore Babylon. With this description complete, the saints are warned to come out of her, that they be not partakers of her sin, and that they receive not of her plagues.

John finishes the last three chapters on a high and glorious note. He shows the preparation and deliverance of the righteous saints, the marriage supper of the Lamb, the destruction of the wicked, the description of the millennium, the great and wonderful promises to those who overcome, the casting out of Satan and his followers, the judgment, the new heaven and new earth, the descent out of heaven of the new Jerusalem, the beauty, glory, honor, and blessings of the city and those who enter therein, and a reminder that Christ surely shall come quickly.

Much of John's last-days mission of gathering the righteous has to do with the book he has already written, and how it is received. The Book of Revelation has tremendous power. The author's sincere prayer is that what is written about the book has neither added to or taken away from the words of the book. The real gem and pearl is this book of scripture itself.

The author wishes to end with this testimony: during the process of researching and writing this book, he has been filled with an overwhelming sense that God's love is always being manifest. This is especially true as we see the prophesied destructions of the last days fulfilled. If God wept for the pain and sins in the days of Noah (Moses 7:28, 29), then surely, heavenly tears are shed for ours. We must focus on what is delivered through the pain of travail. We see the perfecting of the saints, and the arm of the Lord made bare for their deliverance. The establishment of Zion on earth is coupled with the return of the heavenly Zion. Most gloriously, we rest our faith upon the coming of the King of Kings and Lord of Lords, even Jesus Christ, Amen.

Appendix A
Author's Condensed Interpretive Historical Perspective of the World From the Time of Christ

Christ's Work and Glory

Christ comes and establishes his earthly spiritual kingdom in the midst of Satan's dominion. Most reject the spiritual path to God's kingdom on earth as it is in heaven. Major work begins on both sides of the veil. Christ personally atones for the sins of the world, sets a perfect example, and gains the fullness of power over our two most ominous enemies, *death* and *hell*.

Good and righteous men come to earth. Light begins to break forth in the midst of the darkness. Great inroads are made spiritually, politically, and even geographically. The discovery and colonization of America began. The period is known as the reformation.

Some of the most righteous men ever to live are born and gather to America. A heavenly banner of freedom is established in the U.S. Constitution.

Satan's Dominion

Because of pride, most reject Christ's teachings. Satan uses political power and governmental control to begin to physically banish the Lord's Kingdom on earth. Satan works frantically to try to repair a major breech of Satan's kingdom on earth as it is in hell.

Mimicking the Lord's Kingdom, Satan closes the gap with the great apostasy. After Satan has again achieved political and spiritual control, further inroads are made. The Lord describes this condition as *great* and *abominable*.

Satan's kingdom is shaken. Wars and contention increase as Satan marshals his forces.

Secret societies of evil begin to combine to counteract the work of Christ. Socialistic doctrines in opposition to Christ appear again.

The Rise to Power of the Whore Babylon

Satan seeks a political base. A secretly funded socialist uprising is orches-

Christ's Work and Glory

Prophets of God are called, beginning with Joseph Smith. The Book of Mormon is brought forth, in which the workings of Satan are brought to light. The outline of Christ's spiritual kingdom is given. The Church is established. Christ's political and spiritual kingdoms are here in embryo form. The people have opportunity to accept both.

American patriots begin to wake up. Spiritually, the gospel makes inroads with a worldwide missionary program.

Christ's prophets continually testify. Words of Christ from the Book of Mormon and latter-day scripture testify. In general, the spirit of a deep sleep rests upon the people as they close their eyes and ears and begin to desire to partake of the spoils of Satan's work (Isaiah 29:10).

Satan's Dominion

trated in France. Murder, robbery, and plunder are carried on in a grand scale. Napoleon counters by seeking to grab the political power for himself. The first nationwide socialistic uprising is only partially successful. Erosion of the U.S. Constitution begins. Karl Marx, the false prophet, clearly puts into words the outline of Satan's latter-day kingdom. Secret works of darkness multiply.

In the United States and world, anti-Christ business practices amass wealth and control. Satan seeks and gets control of the money supply. Socialistic practices, with their increased tax burden and loss of personal freedom, begin to appear.

Hate, envy, and strife increase as the world goes to war.

Wealth, power, and influence are used to give birth to Satanic kingdom on earth in the Soviet Union. This is the rise of the first beast. Atheism is the religion, communism/socialism the political doctrine. The Great and Abominable is once again on earth. Murder, robbery, and plunder are carried out on a grand scale.

Wickedly and secretly, wealth and power combine; this eventually forms the National Socialists German Workers Party (NAZI). As the socialists rise to power in Germany, murder,

APPENDIX A   153

Christ's Work and Glory

Satan's Dominion

robbery, and plunder are carried on in a worldwide scale.

There is a world movement to unite all under a socialistic, nonrepresentative, tyrannical leadership. The promise is world peace in trade for national sovereignty. A voice and legitimacy are given to the communists. This movement is the rise of the second beast.

Through tribulation, Christ speaks to his people, calling them out of Babylon, inviting all to prepare and come to the wedding supper of the Lamb.

Satan's Influence Increases Under Communism and Socialism Communism

Through revolution, bloodshed, robbery, murder, plunder, and force, the chains of slavery are attached.

Socialism

Inroads against free agency continue. All 10 planks of the Marxist/Satanist doctrine are incorporated into the U.S. system, bypassing the Constitution. People are kept asleep as chains of destruction and slavery are fastened. The spiritual doctrine of Christ is destroyed by worldliness and materialism. Through governmental control, robbery, murder, and plunder are legitimized. Effort is made to unite all into a great and abominable government and social order: The NEW WORLD ORDER.

Appendix B
Author's Interpretive Chronology of Some Signs and Events Prophesied from the Revelation of St. John

Premortal war in heaven between good and evil started there and continued here on earth. (Revelation 12:7-9, 12)

Establishment of Christ's church is identified as those trying to bring the kingdom of God on earth as it is in heaven. (JST 12:7)

Man Child (Christ) comes to the church, which is represented as the woman. (JST 12:3)

Man Child is exalted to the throne of God. (JST 12:3)

Dragon persecutes the woman (Church) (JST 12:13)

Church flees into wilderness (Americas), where it is nourished from the face of serpent for 350 years (author's interpretation) (JST 12:14)

Gospel restored through an angel (14:6)

Prophet and 12 apostles are to be found on the earth. (18:2)

Rise of the false prophet (16:13; 19:20), the satanic gospel of Karl Marx is taught to all the earth.

Whore Babylon amasses unprecedented power. A huge, mysterious satanic force first corrupts, then controls the kings of the earth. (chapter 17)

Rise of first beast, communists/socialists, especially Soviets rise in power (13:1-4) The beast is a creature of the whore Babylon. (17:3)

Rise of the second beast (13:11-14) An earthly force of wonderful power (able to call down fire from heaven is the sight of men). Has a dual division of power (two horns). Has an image like a lamb (peaceable). Speaks as a Dragon (with force, power, and deception). It is a tool of Satan to give a voice to the first beast. Causes them that dwell on earth to worship the first beast (support financially, give legitimacy, learn the doctrines of). The United Nations fits this description.

Power given to the image of the beast (13:14) The rise and power of socialism.

Mark of the beast given (13:15-18) Those having the mark of the image of the beast and worshipping his image are worthy of destruction.

One head of 1st beast wounded unto death (13:14; 17:18) Communism is dead as judged by the appearance of its head.

144,000 specially called, sealed, and endowed servants (chapter 7) called out of tribulation. Do not suffer from the 5th plague. Sing a new song and redeemed from the earth (14:3-5)

Start of the seven plagues (chapters 8-9)
  First plague, conventional warfare. (8:7)
  Second plague, use of weapons of mass destruction on the sea. (8:8-9)
  Third plague, use of weapons of mass destruction on the land (8:10-11); major deaths caused by contamination, not impact.
  Fourth plague, aftermath of warfare, especially the darkening of the sky. (8:13-14)
  Fifth plague, rise of satanic angel from the bottomless pit (9:1-13) uses a green movement campaign to hold miserable, uneasy peace for 5 months (9:3-6). Has power over all except those sealed by Christ (9:4) Uses helicopters as an enforcement tool. (9:7-10)

Saints called out of Babylon (chapter 18)

Destruction of Whore Babylon by the beast (17:16) Heaven and the Holy Apostles rejoice. (18:20)

Saints begin to gather and prepare for wedding supper of the Lamb (19:7-9)
  Sixth plague, beast and 10 kings gather to fight against the Lord's people. (9:14-2) (17:11-14) 200 million soldiers gather. (9:16) One-third of all men killed (9:18) Destroyed when they make war with Lamb (17:14)
  Seventh plague, final harvest of the earth before the millennium (14:19-20; 19:11) Satan bound (Rev 20:2)

New heaven and new earth. Earth violently moves into a new terrestrial orbit (6:12-17; 16:20; 21:1)

Return to earth of Enoch's Zion and Melchizedek's Salem (21:2-3; 11:19)

Christ begins his 1000-year reign (20:4)

Resurrection (20:13)

Satan loosed for a little season at the end of the millennium (20:7-8)

Final Judgment (20:12)

Earth Receives Celestial Glory (chapter 21)

"And he shall reign forever and ever, amen."

Appendix C
Satan's Control vs. God's Agency and Protection

Lucifer's "Ifs" to Gain Control	Christ's "Truth" to Make Us Free
A. If I can *control* the money, I can *control* the nation. Planks #2 & 5 Communist Manifesto	"Ye cannot serve both God and mammon" (Matthew 6:24). "The love of money is the root of all evil" (1 Timothy 6:10). "Ye have sold yourselves for naught, and ye shall be redeemed without money" (3 Nephi 20:38). "If they labor for money, they shall perish" (2 Nephi 26:31). Come ye out of Babylon (Revelation 18). The Law of Consecration given to establish independence of the Church above all under the Celestial World (D & C 78:14). No state shall make anything but gold and silver coin to tender payment of debt (Article 1, Section 8, U.S. Constitution).
B. If I can *control* the media, I can *control* the way people think. Plank #6 Communist Manifesto	"Learn of Me" (Matthew 11:29). "The Holy Spirit for their guide, and have not been deceived" (D & C 45:57). "Search the scriptures: . . . they . . . testify of me" (John 5:39). "A prophet shall the Lord your God raise up" (Acts 3:22-23). No law abridging freedom of speech or press or right of peaceable assembly (1st Amendment, U.S. Constitution).
C. If I can *control* their schools I can *control* their children. Plank #10 Communist Manifesto	"Thou shalt teach them diligently unto thy children . . . in thine house" (Deuteronomy 6:7). "Trust no one to be your teacher nor your minister, except he be

a man of God" (Mosiah 23:14). Parents to teach children in Zion (D & C 68:25). "Establish a house . . . of prayer, . . . fasting, . . . faith, . . . learning, . . . glory, . . . order, a house of God" (D & C 88:119). Congress shall make no law respecting an establishment of religion or prohibiting the free exercise thereof (1st Amendment, U.S. Constitution). This freedom has been taken from our children as they attend public school. In mandatory government schools, the religion of Karl Marx (socialism, secular humanism, and materialism) is freely taught, while prayer and the gospel of Christ are banned.

D. If I can *control* the food, I can *control* the people.
    Planks #6-9, Communist Manifesto

"The revelation to store food may be as essential to our temporal salvation today as boarding the ark was to the people in the days of Noah" (Ezra Taft Benson, Conference Report, Oct. 1973). "If ye are prepared ye shall not fear" (D & C 38:30). "Why call me, Lord, Lord, and do not the things which I say?" (Luke 6:46). Should the Lord decide to cleanse the Church —and the need for that cleansing seems to be increasing—a famine in this land of one years duration could wipe out a large percentage of slothful members, including some ward and stake officers" (Ibid, ETBCR Oct, 1973).

E. If I can *control* the guns I can *control* the property.
  Planks #1, 4, Communist Manifesto

Saints to be armed with righteousness (1 Nephi 14:14). "It may be that the saints will have to beat their plows into swords. It will not do for men to sit down and see their women and children destroyed patiently" (Joseph Smith, May 12, 1844). "Put on the whole armour of God" (Ephesians 6:11). Title of liberty maintained by Christians coming together with their armor (Alma 46). A well-regulated militia being *necessary* to the security of a free state. The right to keep and bear arms shall not be infringed (2nd Amendment, U.S. Constitution).

Author's Note
It is better to die a free man with your weapon in your hand than like a dog without one. This lesson is taught by the socialist/communists, but learned too late by 6 million Jews, 40 million Russians, and 60 million Chinese who were slaughtered. Remember that the shot heard round the world from Concord was fired because of a British attempt at GUN CONTROL."

F. If I can *control* their property, I can *control* everything.
  Plank #1, Communist Manifesto

"And for this purpose have I established the Constitution" (D & C 101:80)

G. If I control everything, I sit as God to rule upon this earth.

Planks of Communist manifesto:

1. Abolition of property in land and application of all rents of land to public purposes.
2. A heavy progressive or graduated income tax.
3. Abolition of all right of inheritance.
4. Confiscation of the property of all emigrants and rebels.
5. Centralization of credit in the hands of the state by means of a national bank with state capital and an exclusive monopoly.
6. Centralization of the means of communication and transport in the hands of the state.
7. Extension of factories and instruments of production owned by the state; the bringing into cultivation of waste lands, and the improvement of the soil generally in accordance with a common plan.
8. Equal obligation of all to work. Establishment of industrial armies, especially for agriculture.
9. Combination of agriculture with manufacturing industries; gradual

"Powers of heaven cannot be controlled only upon the principles of righteousness" (D & C 121:36). When men exercise control over the souls of men, the heavens withdraw (D & C 121:37). Governments must frame laws that secure the rights and control of property (D & C 134:2). See the entirety of the original U.S. Constitution. A heavenly banner!

"Wherefore, because that Satan rebelled against me, and sought to destroy the agency of man, which I, the Lord God, had given him, and also, that I should give unto him mine own power; by the power of mine Only Begotten, I caused that he should be cast down" (Moses 4:3).

abolition of the distinction between town and country by a more equable distribution of the population over the country.

10. Free education for all children in public schools. Abolition of child factory labor in its present form. Combination of education with industrial production, etc.

Note: Socialism and Communism have identical goals. Only the tactics used to bring them about differ. Socialism creeps in by the voice and will of a deceived people. The republic talked about by our forefathers, in which God was the supreme law, is replaced by democracy, where man is. Communism espouses revolution and force as the means to achieving the above goals. "And he became Satan, yea, even the devil, the father of all lies, to deceive and to blind men, and to lead them captive at his will, even as many as would not hearken unto my voice" (Moses 4:4).

"We here in the United States, in converting our government into a social welfare state, have ourselves adopted much of socialism. Specifically, we have to an alarming degree adopted the use of the power of the state in the control and distribution of the fruits of industry. We are on notice, according to the words of the President [of the U.S.] that we're going much further, for he is quoted as saying: We're going to take all the money we think is unnecessarily being spent and take it from the "haves" and give it to the "have-nots!" (1964 Congressional Record, p. 6142). That is the spirit of socialism: we're going to take. The spirit of the United Order is: we're going to give. We have also come a long way on the road to public ownership and management of the vital means of production. In both these areas, the free agency of Americans has been greatly abridged" (Elder Marion G. Romney, Era, June 1966, p. 536).

"However, notwithstanding my abhorrence of it, I am persuaded that socialism is the wave of the present and of the foreseeable future. It has already taken over, or is contending for control in most nations" (Ibid.).

We have been taught that Satan has no power over man except as we allow him to do so. The same is true for nations as well as individuals. Satan rules only because we allow him this power until the flaxen cord is replaced by the chains of hell.

Appendix D
An Enemy Hath Done This: The Threat to Our Freedom

In chapter 2 of President Benson's book, *An Enemy Hath Done This,* (Parliament Publishers, SLC, Utah, 1969), is an excellent treatment of the subject of our freedom. President Benson teaches the pillars on which freedom rests, and by whom they are threatened:

> These abundant blessings have come to us through an economic system which rests largely on three pillars:
> 1. Free enterprise, . . . the right to venture, . . . the right to choose.
> 2. Private property, . . . the right to own.
> 3. A market economy, . . . the right to exchange.
>
> (p. 24)

Yet these basic American beliefs, principles, and attitudes are threatened today as never before.

By whom are they threatened? These basic concepts are threatened by three groups:

1. They are threatened by well-meaning but uninformed people who see the shortcomings of our economic system and believe they can legislate them out of existence. They try to reach the promised land by passing laws. They do not understand our economic system and its limitations. They would load it down with burdens it was never intended to carry. As their schemes begin to break down, more and more controls must be supplied. Patch is placed upon patch, regulation is added to regulation and ultimately, by degree, freedom is lost—without our desiring to lose it and without our knowing why or how it was lost.

2. Our heritage of freedom is threatened by another group—self-seeking men who see in government legislation a way to obtain special privileges for themselves or to restrain their competitors. They use demagoguery as a smokescreen to deceive. These people have no love for freedom or enterprise. They would bargain away their birthright for a mess of pottage. They would learn the value of freedom only after it was gone.

3. A third, still much smaller group is dedicated to the overthrow of the economic and social system that is our tradition. Their philosophy does not stem from Jefferson, but is foreign to our shores. It is a total philosophy of life, atheistic, and utterly opposed to all that we hold dear as a great Christian nation. These men understand our system thoroughly—and they hate it thoroughly. They enlist innocent but willing followers from the uninformed and the unprincipled. Through rabble-rousing and demagoguery they play upon the economic reverses and hardships of the unsuspecting. They promise the impossible, and call black white, and mislead with fallacies masqueraded as truth.

If we lose our freedom, it will be to this strange and unlike coalition of the well-intentioned, the slothful, and the subversives.

It will be because we did not care enough—because we were not alert enough—because we were too apathetic to take note while the precious waters of our God-given freedom slipped—drop by drop—down the drain.

(pp. 25-26)

Also in the same chapter, President Benson quotes this warning from Tom Anderson:

As American businessmen you must stand up and be counted—else you'll be counted out. . . . The middle of the road between the extremes of good and evil is evil. When freedom is at stake, your silence is not golden, it's yellow. . . . Why change the American system which produced the greatest freedom for the greatest number of people in human history, along with the world's highest standard of living, for socialism. . . . Under any name Socialism has been a miserable failure for 1,000 years. . . . *A government big enough to give you everything you want is big enough to take everything you've got.*

(p. 19)

From chapter 3, of this book, President Benson lists the ways in which this destruction is being carried out:

Our Republic and Constitution are being destroyed while enemies of freedom are being aided. How? In ten ways:

1. By diplomatic recognition and aid, and trade and negotiations with the communists.

2. By disarmament of our military defenses.

3. By destruction of our security laws and the promotion of atheism by decisions of the Supreme Court.
4. By loss of sovereignty and solvency through international commitments and membership in world organizations.
5. By undermining of local law enforcement agencies and Congressional investigating committees.
6. By usurpations by the executive and judicial branches of our federal government.
7. By lawlessness in the name of civil rights.
8. By a staggering national debt with inflation and a corruption of the currency.
9. By a multiplicity of executive orders and federal programs which greatly weaken local and state governments.
10. By the sacrifice of American manhood by engaging in wars we apparently have no intention of winning.

(p. 40)

One way we give up our freedom is through the growing trend for government to license, permit, restrict, and regulate more and more aspects of our lives. This is done under the auspices of protecting the public, but usually the result is the protection of a privileged few, at the expense of the public. These government-protected monopolies then invest heavily for the continuance of this privilege. The net result is a guarantee that their way of doing something will forever be the way it will be done, now mandated by law. Innovation, creativity, and the independent spirit is thus stifled.

President McKay has counseled us against prohibiting others from pursuing the occupation of their choice. He said:

> It is a great imposition, if indeed not a crime, for any government, any labor union, or any other organization to deny a man the right to speak, to worship, and to work (*Statements on Communism and the Constitution of the United States,* p. 17.)

The prophet, Joseph Smith, expressed a similar view to the council of the City of Nauvoo:

> I also spoke at length for the repeal of the ordinance of the city licensing merchants, hawkers, taverns, and ordinaries, desiring that this might be a free people, and enjoy equal rights and privileges, and the ordinances were repealed (*History of the Church,* Vol. 6, p. 8).

The only justification for governmental licensing is to restrict something that would otherwise be constitutionally illegal. All other infringements are usurpation. One should not need governmental permission to do that which the God-given constitution already guarantees the right to do, i.e. pursue life, liberty, or happiness without infringing upon the rights of others.

Bibliography

1964 Congressional Record

The 1994 Guiness Book of World Records. New York: Bantam Nonfiction/ Guiness Publishing LTD, 1994.

Allen, Gary. *None Dare Call It Conspiracy*. Seal Beach, CA: Concord Press, 1971.

Andersen, H. Verlan. *The Great and Abominable Church of the Devil*. Orem, Utah.

Barton, David. *America, to Pray or Not to Pray*. Aledo, Texas: Wall Builders Press, 1988.

Benson, Ezra Taft. "I Testify." *Ensign*, November, 1988.

Benson, Ezra Taft. *Teachings of Ezra Taft Benson*. Salt Lake City: Bookcraft, 1988.

Benson, Ezra Taft. Conference Report, October 1968.

Benson, Ezra Taft. Conference Report, October 1973.

Benson, Ezra Taft. *God, Family, Country*. Salt Lake City: Deseret Book, 1974.

Benson, Ezra Taft. "The Savior's Visit to America." *Ensign*, May 1987.

Benson, Ezra Taft. *Ensign*, September 1987.

Benson, Ezra Taft. *The Red Carpet, Socialism—the Royal Road to Communism*. Salt Lake City: Bookcraft, 1962.

Benson, Ezra Taft. Conference Report, October 1961.

Benson, Ezra Taft. *An Enemy Hath Done This*. Compiled by Jerrald L. Newquist. Salt Lake City: Parliament Publishers, 1969.

Benson, Ezra Taft. Conference Report, April 1963.

Bible

Book of Mormon

Browder, Earl. *Victory and After*. New York International Publishers, 1942.

Congressional Record, December 22, 1913 (Vol. 51).

Doctrine & Covenants

Epperson, A. Ralph. *The Unseen Hand*. Tucson, Arizona: Publius Press, 1985.

Goldwater, Barry. *With No Apologies*. NY: William Morrow and Co., 1980.

Grant, Heber J. and McKay, David O. *Messages of the First Presidency (Vol. 6)*.

Grantfuller, John. *The Day We Bombed Utah*. New York: New American Library, 1984.

Griffin, G. Edward. *The Creature from Jekyll Island, A Second Look at the Federal Reserve*. Appleton, WI: American Opinion, 1994.

Hansen, L. Taylor. *He Walked the Americas*. Amherst, WI: Amherst Press, 1963.

Jacob, Carl H. *Superbombs, Saints and Scriptures*. Salt Lake City: Deseret Book, 1960.

Journal of Discourses, Volumes 1, 5, 8, 13, 14, 15, 19, 22, 23, 24.

Kimball, Spencer W. *Teachings of Spencer W. Kimball*. Edited by Edward L. Kimball. Salt Lake City: Bookcraft, 1982.

King, Alexander, and Schneider, Bertrand. *The First Global Revolution*. New York: Pantheon Books, 1991.

Lee, Robert W. *The United Nations Conspiracy*, Belmont, MA: Western Islands, 1981.

Lee, Harold B. *Stand Ye in Holy Places*. Salt Lake City: Deseret Book, 1974.

Marx, Karl. *Communist Manifesto*.

Maziarz, Edward A., and Greenwood, Thomas. *Greek Mathematical Philosophy*. New York: Frederick Ungar Publishing Co., 1968.

McConkie, Bruce R. Conference Report, April 1979.

McConkie, Bruce R. *Doctrinal New Testament Commentary (Vol III)*. Salt Lake City: Bookcraft, 1973.

McKay, David O. *Improvement Era*, June 1966.

McKay, David O. *Statements on Communism and the Constitution of the United States*. Salt Lake City: Deseret Book, 1964.

McKay, David O. *Gospel Ideals*. Salt Lake City: Deseret Book, 1953.

Newquist, Jerrald. *Prophets, Principles, and National Survival*. Salt Lake City: Publishers Press, 1964.

Nibley, Hugh. *Brigham Counsels the Saints*. Salt Lake City: Deseret Book, 1994.

Pearl of Great Price

Perloff, James. *The Shadows of Power*. Appleton, WI: Western Islands, 1988.

Quigley, Carroll. *Tragedy and Hope, A History of the World in Our Time*. New York: Macmillan Co., 1966.

Romney. Marion G. *Improvement Era*, June 1966.

Sampson, Joe. *Written by the Finger of God*. Sandy, Utah: Wellspring Publishing, 1993.

Sanders, Carl. Transcript from speech at the Preparedness Fair Expo '93, Phoenix, Arizona.

Skousen, W. Cleon. *The Naked Capitalist*. Salt Lake City: Author, 1970.

Skousen, W. Cleon. *The Naked Communist*. Salt Lake City: The Ensign Publishing Co., 1958.

Smith, Joseph. *Lectures on Faith*.

Smith, Joseph Fielding. *Answers to Gospel Questions (Vol. 4)*. Salt Lake City: Deseret Book, 1979.

Smith, Joseph Fielding. *Doctrines of Salvation (Vol. 1)*. Salt Lake City: Bookcraft, 1954.

Smith, Joseph Fielding. *The Progress of Man*. Salt Lake City: Deseret Book, 1964.

Smith, Joseph F. *History of the Church*. Salt Lake City: Deseret Book, 1951.

Smith, Joseph Fielding. *Teachings of the Prophet Joseph Smith*. Salt Lake City: Deseret Book, 1976.

Strong, James. *Strong's Exhaustive Concordance of the Bible*. Nashville, Tenn.: Thomas Nelson Publishers.

Taylor, John. *Times and Seasons (Vol. 5)*. Navuoo: December 15, 1844.

Time Magazine, April 16, 1945.

The U.S. Constitution.

Selected Addional Recommended Reading

Scripture Commentary

Adams, L. Lamar. *The Living Message of Isaiah*. Salt Lake City: Deseret Book, 1981.

Crowther, Duane S. *Prophecy, Key to the Future*. Salt Lake City: Bookcraft, 1962.

Draper, Richard D. *Opening the Seven Seals*. Salt Lake City: Deseret Book, 1991.

Gileadi, Avraham. *The Book of Isaiah*. Sake Lake City: Deseret Book, 1988.

Gileadi, Avraham. *The Last Days*. Salt Lake City: Covenant, 1991.

Lund, Gerald N. *The Coming of the Lord*. Salt Lake City: Bookcraft, 1971.

McConkie, Bruce R. *The Millennial Messiah*. Salt Lake City: Deseret Book, 1982.

Nibley, Hugh. *Approaching Zion*. Salt Lake City: Deseret Book, 1989.

Nibley, Hugh, *The Prophetic Book of Mormon*. Salt Lake City: Deseret Book, 1989.

Nyman, Monte S. *The Words of Jeremiah*. Salt Lake City: Bookcraft, 1982.

Robinson, Stephen E. *Believing Christ*. Salt Lake City: Deseret Book, 1992.

Skousen, W. Cleon. *Prophecy and Modern Times*. Salt Lake City: Ensign Publishing, 1988.

Talmage, James E. *Jesus the Christ*. London: Church of Jesus Christ of Latter-day Saints, 1962.

Political Commentary for Today

Allison, Andrew M., Richard Maxfield, K. DeLynn Cook, and W. Cleon Skousen, *The Real Thomas Jefferson*, 2nd ed., Washington, DC: National Center for Constitutional Studies, 1983.

Andersen, H. Verlan. *Many Are Called but Few Are Chosen*. Orem, Utah, 1967.

Bastiat, Frederic. *The Law*, NY: Foundation for Economic Education, 1950.

Crowther, Duane S. *America, God's Chosen Land of Liberty.* Bountiful, UT: Horizon Publishers, 1987.

Golitsyn, Anatoliy. *New Lies for Old.* NY: Pidd, Mead and Co., 1984.

Grammer, Joseph W. *Awake and Arise.* Salt Lake City: Northwest Publishers, 1993.

Hamilton, Alexander, James Madison, and John Jay, *The Federalist Papers.* Reprinted by New American Library, NY, 1961.

Jasper, William F. *Global Tyranny . . . Step by Step, the United Nations and the Emerging New World Order.* Appleton, WI: Western Islands, 1992.

Marrs, Texe. *Millennium.* Austin, TX: Living Truth Publishers, 1990.

McAlvany, Don. *Towards a New World Order.* Durango, CO: McAlvany Intelligence Advisor, 1993.

Mullins, Eustice. *Secrets of the Federal Reserve.* Staunton, VA: Bankers Research Institute, 1983.

Nicolov, Nicola M. *The World Conspiracy.* Portland, OR: Author, 1990.

Report from Iron Mountain on the Possibility and Desirability of Peace. NY: Dial Press, 1967.

Schlesinge, Jr. *The Age of Jackson.* NY: Mentorbooks, 1945.

Skousen, W. Cleon. *The Making of America, the Substance and Meaning of the Constitution.* Washington, DC: National Center for Constitutional Studies, 1985.

Sutton, Antony C. *National Suicide: Military Aid to the Soviet Union.* NY: Arlington House, 1973.

The United States Constitution and Bill of Rights

Williams, Lindsey. *To Seduce a Nation.* Kasilof, AK: Worth Publishing, 1989.

Special Helps for Preparedness

Essentials of Home Production and Storage, Salt Lake City: LDS Distribution Center.

Bubbel, Frederick W. *On the Wings of Faith.* Salt Lake City: Bookcraft, 1972.

Crockett, Barry G. and Lynette B. *A Year's Supply.* Salt Lake City: Publishers Press, 1988.

Hershey, Tom. *Hiroshima.* NY: Bantam Books, 1946.

Kearny, Cresson H. *Nuclear War Survival Skills*. Cave Junction, OR: Oregon Institute of Science and Medicine, 1987.

LeBaron, Wayne D. *The Reluctant Survivors, A Family Guide to the Prevention and Treatment of Radiation Sickness*. Salt Lake City: Dream Garden Press, 1984.

Robinson, Arthur and North, Gary. *Fighting Chance, Ten Feet to Survival*. Cave Junction, OR: Oregon Institute of Science and Medicine, 1986.

Schechter, Steven R. *Fighting Radiation and Chemical Pollutants with Foods, Herbs, and Vitamins*. Encinitas CA: Vitality, Ink., 1988.

Tenney, Louise. *Today's Herbal Health*. Provo, Utah: Woodland Books, 1983.

Index

A

Abominable Church, 19, 51, 52, 74, 132, 151
Abraham, 114.
Adam-ondi-Ahman, 54, 55.
All given to righteous, 142.
America, church flees to, 78, 155.
Animals, partake of salvation, 32, 33.
Apocalypse, definition of, 11.
Armageddon, 119.
Atonement of Christ, 38, 39, 45, 47.

B

Babylon, 120, 121, 127, 148, 154, 158.
   destruction of, 132-138, 155.
Banking, monopolistic centralized, 119, 120, 123, 124, 131.
Beast, first beast, scarlet beast, 11, 70, 84, 85, 90, 125, 128, 132, 133, 138, 140, 154, 147.
   image, mark and number of, 97, 98, 101-104, 108, 110, 113, 117, 131, 133, 138, 148.
   second, 87, 90, 133, 148, 149, 155.
   wounding and healing of, 86, 132, 148, 149, 155.
Beheaded, witnesses of Jesus are, 139.
Benson, Ezra Taft
   Book of Mormon, 21, 68.
   Communism and Socialism have same effect, 100, 110.
   conspiracy fact, 130.
   endorses book *None Dare Call It Conspiracy*, 130.
   power of government from people, 96.
   Social Security unconstitutional, 99.
   stands for freedom, 139.
Bethel, 115.
Bitter herb, 56, 57.
Blasphemy, 85.
Book, mission for John, 65.

Book of Revelation
   connected to Book of Mormon, 21, 146.
   for today, 8, 9, 10.
   for us, 9, 21.
   foretells future events, 9, 21, 84.
   plainest book, 11, 19, 20, 146.
Bottomless pit, 139.

C

Calling and election, 28, 43, 44.
Caught up, righteous are, 48, 73, 75, 115, 116.
Chain, Satanic symbol, 48, 139.
Chernobyl is wormwood, 56.
Children, 34, 47, 48, 138.
City of God, 26, 28, 70, 72, 143, 144.
Clark, J. Reuben, U.N. Charter is a war document, 89.
Coded message, 146.
Comings of Christ, 67-69.
   quickly, 144.
   to a prepared people, 19, 44, 67, 138.
Communism, 85, 89, 91-95, 99, 100, 107, 110, 117, 118, 128-130, 132, 147-149.
Constitution, 96, 99, 107, 114, 123, 150, 152, 158-160.
Cubic, Holy City from heaven is, 143.

D

Daniel, 132-135.
Deception of whole earth, 77, 84, 129, 139, 146.

E

Earth, 49, 112.
Earthquake(s), 40, 43, 54, 119.
Elias, John is, 66, 112.
Enoch, 45, 50, 72, 112, 114, 116, 129, 141, 142, 155.
Euphrates River, 62, 118.

INDEX

F

Federal Reserve, 122, 123, 124, 126.
Food storage, 36, 159.
Fornication, 27, 28, 51, 133, 134.
Four winds, 42-44.

G

Goldwater, Barry, discusses Trilateralists, 119.
Gorbachev, Mikhail, head of International Green Cross, 61.
Grant, Heber J., Communism, Nazism, Fascism, 93.
Green movement, 61, 155.
Guiness Book of World Records, communist murders cited, 85.

H

Helicopter, John seems to describe, 62.

I

Income tax, 124.
Iodine 131, 58, 59.

J

Jackson, Andrew, abolished Second National Bank, 124.
Jacob, 114-116.
Jerusalem, 70-73, 114, 116, 142.
Joshua, type of Christ at Last Days, 64.

K

Kimball, Spencer W., on Socialism, 95.
Kingdom of God is political and spiritual, 22, 74, 76, 132, 152.
Kings and priests unto God, 22.

L

Last Days shortened, 62, 63.
Lee, Harold B., United Order not Socialistic or Communistic, 95.
Licensing, 166.
Lindbergh, Charles, Sr. Congressman, 123.
Lord's day, 22, 23.

M

Manifesto, Communist, 158-161.
Marx, Karl, 82, 85, 118, 152, 154.
Martyrs, 24, 111, 127, 128, 140 149.
McConkie, Bruce R.
  atomic holocausts, 58.
  plagues could be atomic warfare, 58.
  scarlet beast communism? 107.
McFadden, Louis, Congressman, 123.
McKay, David O.
  admonish to read Naked Communist, 130.
  Communism diametrically opposed to gospel, 118.
  communistic ideas anti-Christ, 94.
  free agency is measuring rod, 97.
  position of Church on communism, 86.
  right to speak, worship, work, 165.
  Satan plans to destroy freedom, 120.
  Supreme Court misinterprets 1st admendment, 53.
Media, 71, 158.
Melchizedek, 74, 75, 114, 141, 155.
Microchip, 102, 103.
Money, 125, 136, 152, 158.

N

Naked Communist, 130.
Naked Capitalist, 130.
Nazi, 93.
New heaven, 41, 155.
New Jerusalem, 26, 28, 73, 113, 135, 142.
New World Order, 119, 153.
Noah—Last Days compared to, 8, 50, 129, 150.
None Dare Call It Conspiracy, 130.
Notarikon, 105, 106.
Nuclear destruction, 55-60, 104, 117, 135.

O

One hundred forty-four thousand, 43, 44, 66, 67, 109, 112, 148, 155.

P

Pilgrims, 78.
Plagues, 44, 54, 55, 57-60, 113, 116, 146, 155.
Pratt, Orson
  priesthood purified in temple, 44.
  two cities caught up, 73.

Prayer in America, 52, 53.
Premortal war, 76, 84, 147, 154.
Pride, 60, 80, 91. 107, 128.
Proxy, 38, 39.

Q

Quigley, Carroll, Professor, 130.

R

Rod of Iron, 25, 28, 77.
Romney, Marion G., Communism and Socialism, 160, 161.

S

Sacrifice required, 10, 37, 38, 140, 54, 110.
Sanders, Carl P., Dr., 102-105.
Satan
  cast to earth, 76, 77.
  morning star, 84.
  robs agency, 84, 94, 99, 129.
Sea, earth no longer has, 141.
Sea of Glass, 30, 113.
Seal, representing 1000-year periods, 35, 41, 113.
Seal of God on foreheads, 43, 44, 62.
Second Comforter, 28.
Secret works, combinations, 46, 90, 91, 122, 126, 128-132, 137, 145, 151.
Seven churches, 23, 24.
Seven plagues, order and nature of, 53-58, 155.
Seven thousand years, 33, 35.
Seven trumpets, 64.
Silence, half-hour of, 51, 52.
Six thousand years, 23, 53.
Skousen, Cleon, 130.
Smith, George Albert, do not covet, 93.
Smith, Joseph
  on Socialism, 91.
  144,000 saviors on Mount Zion, 44.
  repeal of licensing laws, 166.
Smith, Joseph F., gain not at expense of others, 93.
Smith, Joseph Fielding, dictatorship—modern trend, 94.
Snow, Lorenzo, United Order based on free will, 92.
Social security number, 97-99.
Socialism, evil and ineffective, 79-82, 91, 95, 96, 99, 101, 110, 125, 129, 148, 151-153.
Sodom and Gomorrah, similar to our day, 75.
Sorceries and witchcraft, 63, 136.

T

TRSQ, 106.
Tabernacle, 50, 72, 114, 141.
Talent—hail stone, weight of, 121.
Tares, 51, 66.
Taylor, John
  judge system by fruits, 80.
  on Communism, 92.
  socialists in Nauvoo, 80, 81.
Temple(s), 28, 43, 70, 73, 116, 143.
Third Nephi parallels our day, 68.
Three hundred fifty years, Church is nourished for, 78, 155.
Throne of God, 30, 144.
Time, no longer, 64, 65.
Travail, destruction comes like, 8, 104, 150.
Tribulation, coming out of, 45, 48-50, 153.
Trilateralist, 119.
Two hundred million, army of, 62, 138.
Two witnesses/prophets, 70, 71.

U

United Nations, 87-89, 148.

United Order, 92, 95.
Urim and Thummim, 25, 28, 113.

W

Welfare state, 100, 102.
White linen, 141.
Whore, great, 52, 122, 127, 128, 132, 133, 137, 149, 154.
Wine of fornication, 122, 125, 126.
Woodruff, Wilford, free agency from God, 92.

Word of God, 25, 28.
Wormwood, 56, 57.

Y

Year 2000, speculation concerning, 66.
Young, Brigham, on socialism, 91.

Z

Zion, establishment of, 8, 45, 48, 49, 50, 75, 113, 115, 116 141, 146, 150.